V. S. NAIPAUL

LITERATURE AND LIFE: BRITISH WRITERS

Selected list of titles in the series:

Anthony Burgess	Samuel Coale
Noel Coward	Robert F. Kiernan
Arthur Conan Doyle	Don Richard Cox
T. S. Eliot	Burton Raffel
Ford Madox Ford	Sondra J. Stang
E. M. Forster	Claude J. Summers
Oliver Goldsmith and Richard Brinsley Sheridan	Marlies K. Danziger
Robert Graves	Katherine Snipes
Graham Greene	Richard Kelly
Aldous Huxley	Guinevera A. Nance
Christopher Isherwood	Claude J. Summers
James Joyce	Bernard Benstock
Christopher Marlowe	Gerald Pinciss
Katherine Mansfield	Rhoda B. Nathan
John Masefield	June Dwyer
W. Somerset Maugham	Archie K. Loss
Barbara Pym	Robert Emmet Long
Jean Rhys	Arnold E. Davidson
Shakespeare's Comedies	Jack A. Vaughn
Shakespeare's Histories	George J. Becker
Shakespeare's Tragedies	Phyllis Rackin
Muriel Spark	Velma Bourgeois Richmond
Tom Stoppard	Felicia Londré
J. R. R. Tolkien	Katharyn W. Crabbe
Evelyn Waugh	Katharyn W. Crabbe
Oscar Wilde	Robert Keith Miller
Virginia Woolf	Manly Johnson
William Butler Yeats (Plays)	Anthony Bradley
The Poetry of William Butler Yeats	William H. O'Donnell

Complete list of titles in the series available from the publisher on request. Some titles are also in paperback.

V. S. NAIPAUL

Richard Kelly

A Frederick Ungar Book
CONTINUUM • NEW YORK

1989

The Continuum Publishing Company
370 Lexington Avenue
New York, NY 10017

Printed in the United States of America

Library of Congress Cataloging-in-Publication Data

Kelly, Richard Michael, 1937–
V.S. Naipaul / Richard Kelly.
p. cm. — (Literature and life. British writers)
"A Frederick Ungar book."
Bibliography: p.
Includes index.
ISBN 0-8264-0418-9
1. Naipaul, V. S. (Vidiadhar Surajprasad), 1932– . 2. Authors, Trinidadian—20th century—Biography. 3. Developing countries in literature. I. Title. II. Series.
PR9272.9.N32Z747 1989
823′.914—dc19
[B] 88-27414
CIP

Contents

Chronology

1932 Born in Chaguanas, Trinidad, August 17.
1948 Wins Trinidad government scholarship to study abroad.
1950 Leaves Trinidad to study literature at University College, Oxford.
1955 Marries Patricia Ann Hale.
1956 Makes his first return to Trinidad to visit his family.
1957 Publishes *The Mystic Masseur.*
1958 Publishes *The Suffrage of Elvira.* Awarded the John Llewellyn Rhys Memorial Prize for *The Mystic Masseur.* Reviews fiction for *The New Statesman* until 1961.
1959 Publishes *Miguel Street.*
1960 Returns to Trinidad on a scholarship granted by the government of Trinidad and Tobago; researches and begins writing *The Middle Passage.*
1961 Publishes *A House for Mr. Biswas.* Receives the Somerset Maugham Award for *Miguel Street.*
1962 Publishes *The Middle Passage.* Begins a year-long tour of India during which he gathers material for *An Area of Darkness.*
1963 Publishes *Mr. Stone and the Knights Companion.*
1964 Publishes *An Area of Darkness.* Receives the Hawthornden Prize for *Mr. Stone and the Knights Companion.*
1967 Publishes *The Mimic Men* and *A Flag on the Island.*
1968 Receives the W. H. Smith Prize for *The Mimic Men.*
1969 Publishes *The Loss of El Dorado.*
1970 Returns to England after his travels in the Caribbean, the

United States, and Victoria, British Columbia. Moves into a cottage in Wiltshire.

1971 Publishes *In a Free State.*

1972 Publishes *The Overcrowded Barracoon.*

1975 Publishes *Guerrillas.*

1977 Publishes *India: A Wounded Civilization.*

1978 Teaches at Wesleyan College, Connecticut.

1979 Publishes *A Bend in the River.* Travels to Iran and other Muslim countries in order to research his study *Among the Believers.*

1980 Publishes *The Return of Eva Peron with the Killings in Trinidad.*

1981 Publishes *Among the Believers.*

1984 Publishes *Finding the Center.*

1987 Publishes *The Enigma of Arrival.* Tours the southern United States to research a study of its culture.

1988 Writes *A Turn in the South,* a commentary based upon his tour of the South, scheduled for publication in February, 1989.

V. S. NAIPAUL

1

The World as It Is

Salim, the young Indian narrator of *A Bend in the River,* opens his story with the statement: "The world is what it is; men who are nothing, who allow themselves to become nothing, have no place in it." There are no places to escape to in this changing, dangerous, and disillusioning world; and this is especially true for Third World people. The idea of going home, the idea of the other place, is a deception that "comforted only to weaken and destroy." "We had become what the world outside had made us," Salim concludes; "we had to live in the world as it existed." Salim reflects a central theme in the life and writings of V. S. Naipaul. An intensely restless man, Naipaul has spent much of his adult life traveling about the world, recording the profound but often overlooked tremors and anxieties that threaten one's sense of peace and place. He has peeled back the facade of personal and communal order to reveal chaos and violence. He has exposed the terrifying fragility of life that lies behind the false ideals and seductive dreams of a more perfect home in the past, a safe house in the wood.

At present there are no biographies of Naipaul, though surely in time there will be several. He lives a very private, almost reclusive life in England, and little factual information about him is known. When he does write or talk about his life, he carefully selects incidents or details that are important in terms of his development as a writer. He has given several interviews about his books, his early life in Trinidad, his thoughts on international politics, and his views of other authors. In 1984 he published "Prologue to an Autobiography," which he describes as "not an autobiography, a story of a life or deeds done. It is an account of something less easily seized: my literary beginnings and the imaginative promptings of my many-sided background."

There are many sources, then, from which to construct a preliminary sketch of Naipaul's life, especially the character of his mind and the importance of his childhood to his development as a writer. In *The Enigma of Arrival* (1987) Naipaul attempts to fuse his Caribbean past with his English present. Because of the unique nature of this book—an autobiographical meditation designated a novel—it will be fully discussed in the last chapter of this study. Over the years of writing travel books and novels, Naipaul appears to have come to the realization that all of his writings are essentially autobiographical, that the imaginative structures of his novels—despite their foreign settings and variety of characters—are all built upon the foundations of his personal dreams, fears, and recollections. *The Enigma of Arrival*, then, openly attests to the creative unity of fact and fiction.

Vidiadhar Surajprasad Naipaul was born in Chaguanas, Trinidad, on August 17, 1932, the grandson of a Hindu who had come to the island from Uttar Pradesh in India as an indentured servant. Naipaul's father was intolerant of Hindu rituals and no record was kept of the hour of his son's birth, nor was a horoscope drawn up. Naipaul's first memory is "of waking up in a hospital room and finding myself strapped to the bed."[1] He was two years old at the time and had contracted pneumonia, which, he feels, has probably damaged his health for life.

From earliest childhood Naipaul developed a sense of dislocation. He explains that his early memories are jumbled because "between my birth and the age of seven we lived in about seven or eight different houses. I think it is because one has lived this disordered life that I haven't been able to settle down, even as an adult."[2] Up to age forty he had never lived in any house for more than three and a half years. Naipaul's sense of dislocation is also cultural and historical. After the Act of Emancipation in 1833, India became the main overseas source of cheap labor for the British Caribbean islands. According to Kenneth Ramchand between 1839 and 1917 over 400,000 indentured Indians were imported as substitutes for the freed Negroes. Most of these new slaves, taken from the poverty-stricken districts of India, were transported to Guyana (239,000) and to Trinidad (134,000), where there was a desperate need for laborers.[3] During Naipaul's childhood descendants of Indians comprised approximately one-third of the population of Trinidad. By and large, the Indian community lived apart from the Negroes, the Asians, and the other cultural groups.

According to Naipaul, the Indians tend to live in the country, to work the land, while the Negroes live in the cities. On his return visit to Trinidad in 1960 Naipaul noted the intense rivalry and hatred between the Indians and Negroes. Despite the large population of Indians, their customs and rituals are perceived by fellow islanders as quaint and exotic. Their ties to India, to Islam and Hinduism, have grown vague over the years and now serve mainly to tie the community together in a borrowed, colonial culture. "Living by themselves in villages," Naipaul writes, "the Indians were able to have a complete community life. It was a world eaten up with jealousies and family feuds and village feuds; but it was a world of its own, a community within the colonial society, without responsibility, with authority doubly and trebly removed. Loyalties were narrow: to the family, the village."

Naipaul says that he grew up with two ideas of history: one with dates (such as the history of Rome and that of nineteenth-century England) and his family's history, which had no dates. His ancestors' past in India takes on the quality of myth: "Out of that darkness we had all come. . . . The India from which we had come was impossibly remote, almost imaginary as the land of the *Ramayana*, our Hindu epic. I lived easily with that darkness, that lack of knowledge. I never thought to inquire further." Much later, in 1962, Naipaul traveled to India in search of his mythical past and recorded his impressions in a book appropriately entitled *An Area of Darkness*. He discovered India to be an alien world, an area of darkness still, and his critical commentary on India's failings as a culture stirred up considerable debate. Nevertheless, there were connections made. He met an old woman named Jussodra who knew his grandfather and she recited his genealogy and adventures to him. Although poor, his grandfather left his village to study in Banaras, as Brahmins had done for centuries. There he met a man who told him about a far-off land called Trinidad where there was a need for pundits and teachers. And so he indentured himself for five years and went to

Trinidad, not as a teacher, as he had thought, but as a worker in a sugar factory. He supplemented his salary by doing pundit's work in the evening, married, and began to prosper. He purchased land and built two houses. A restless man, he died during his second trip back to India.

Essentially cut off from Trinidad society as a whole, living within a tightly-knit Indian community in a colonial world, lacking a sense of connection with his Indian heritage, moving with his family from house to house, the young Naipaul felt isolated and adrift. He turned to his father for a sense of direction and for emotional strength. Later, in his novel *A House for Mr. Biswas,* Naipaul would pay homage to his father by making him the model for his hero, Mr. Mohun Biswas.

"The ambition to be a writer was given to me by my father," Naipaul writes. Born in 1906, his father was a journalist for much of his working life, an unusual occupation for a Trinidad Indian of his generation. His connection with the *Trinidad Guardian* mysteriously ceased in 1934, and he worked at odd jobs, moving between his wife's family and the protection of a wealthy uncle. "Poor himself," Naipaul recollects, "with close relations who were still agricultural laborers, my father dangled all his life in a half-dependence and half-esteem between these two powerful families." In 1938 he returned to the *Guardian* as a city reporter and the family (there were five children, three girls and two boys) moved to Port of Spain, to a house owned by Naipaul's maternal grandmother. It was here that Naipaul was introduced to the life of the street, where he discovered the characters for his book *Miguel Street*. It was also here that Naipaul discovered that his father had written pieces of short fiction. They were not especially distinguished fiction but they served to inspire the young boy to become a writer himself.

Armed with the fantasy of nobility that comes with being a writer, Naipaul describes the period in Port of Spain as the serenest time of his childhood. He did not know then that his father was on the brink of a mental breakdown. Naipaul had witnessed his father's rages against his wife's family but learned only later that one day his father looked into the mirror and screamed that he could not see himself. From that day forward the house seemed to hold only terror for him, and so he left it to become a wanderer. For thirteen years he had no house of his own.

His family moved several times after that initial peaceful interlude in Port of Spain, and each move brought with it increasing tension. The family finally moved back to Port of Spain but this time they had to live in a small portion of the house. To make matters worse, many members of Naipaul's mother's family began to move in with them, and life among the extended family became intolerable. Toward the end of 1946, when Naipaul was fourteen, his father managed to buy his own house. "By that time," he recalls, "my childhood was over; I was fully made." His father transmitted to him not only a sense of a vocation as a writer but a fundamental anxiety, a fear of extinction, that only writing could alleviate: "That was his subsidiary gift to me. That fear became mine as well. It was linked with the idea of the vocation: the fear could be combated only by the exercise of the vocation."

There are other aspects of Naipaul's father that he inherited as well. Naipaul admits that as a young boy he hated school because he despised an involvement with other people in groups. He felt that he had to surrender his freedom as an individual. "The little fuse that is within me," he says in an interview, "that protects me from doing terrible things, burns out very quickly, and I withdraw. One is by nature a kind of free-lance, and this might go back to that relationship with my father, to that sense of isolation."[4] Naipaul also acknowledges that his father transmitted to him a feeling of contempt for others: "I was always very critical, liable to too easy a contempt. I think this is something that my father gave to me. My father was a defeated man: I think contempt was all that he could teach me, and I was contaminated by this."[5]

Naipaul traces his father's contempt to the Hindu clan life that he was forced to live among his wife's family. "I grew up with about fifty cousins and that was like a crash course in the world. You learned about cruelty, about propaganda, about the destruction of reputations. You learned about forming allies. It was that kind of background, I think, to which my father was reacting."[6] It was also the kind of world against which Naipaul was reacting. The neutered men, the oppressed and cantankerous women, the uneducated children that filled the rooms in his grandmother's house in Port of Spain gave everyone the desire to break away. The household finally disintegrated but not before it "had released energy in people who might otherwise have remained passive." Many of the cousins acquired professions and wealth and some migrated to other countries. "For all its physical wretchedness and internal tensions, the life of the clan had given us all a start. It had given us a caste certainty, a high sense of the self." Over the years Naipaul learned how to transform the contempt inherited from his father into ironic detachment, an attitude that informs much of his fiction.

Desperately wanting to get away from the claustrophobic pressures of his family and small island life, in 1948 Naipaul sought and won a Trinidad government scholarship. He intended to use his scholarship to study English at Oxford University, not because he wanted the degree but simply to escape from the island. So, in 1950, he left Trinidad to study literature at University College, Oxford. He carried a notebook and a purple pencil with him on the plane trip to New York and on the ship to Southampton. He was going to become a writer. He had great expectations, and the time had come to begin gathering material for his books.

Reflecting on his youthful bravado in *The Enigma of Arrival,* Naipaul does a masterful job of showing how as a young man he was filling his notebook with all of the wrong details about the people around him on his voyage to England. In those early days he had failed to see that the man and the writer were one in the same. He was too eagerly seeking out literary perceptions, "metropolitan material." In so doing he was editing out all of the material that he later came to realize was the essential material of fiction: his humiliations, fears, dreams, the mingling of international peoples in the boardinghouse where he lived before entering Oxford. He had overlooked enormous opportunities but he was learning his craft by trial and error.

He was very lonely in London and his excursions about the city were joyless and ignorant. The London he thought he knew, Dickens's London, was an illusion, a fantasy city that existed only in the author's mind. London turned out to be strange and unknown. To make matters worse, Naipaul now had to abandon the dream that kept his imagination alive and gave him hope for so many years in Trinidad: "I lost the gift of fantasy, the dream of the future, the far-off place where I was going. . . . Now, in the place that for all those years had been the 'elsewhere,' no further dream was possible."

As a young man Naipaul had read such writers as Conrad, Dickens, and the Brontës, and came to Oxford with the expectation that his youthful delight in such exotic authors would be nourished. He quickly realized that his decision to study English at the university was a mistake: "The English course had little to do with literature. It was a 'discipline' aimed at juvenile antiquarians. . . . I had looked forward to wandering among large tracts of writing; I was presented with 'texts.' " He had no taste for scholarship, for tracking the development of literary movements but sought instead to relate literature to life. "Now I discovered that the study of literature had been made scientific, that each writer had to be approached through the booby-traps of scholarship."

Naipaul's aspirations to become a writer were severely tempered not only by his Oxford experiences but by the limited cultural background provided by his native land. Trinidad was a country without a literature, without a clearly defined culture. "It was only our Britishness, our belonging to the British Empire, which gave us any identity," he writes. There were no scientists, engineers, explorers, soldiers, or poets. "The cricketer was our only hero-figure." Living in a borrowed culture, Naipaul later observed, "the West Indian, more than most, needs writers to tell him who he is and where he stands." Believing that a literature can grow only out of a strong framework of social convention, Naipaul recognized that the West Indian knows only his involvement with the white world, a limitation that deprives his work of universal appeal. How, then, does a writer raised in a colonial society, with steel bands and cricket as its claim to fame, manage to proceed?

"To us, without a mythology," Naipaul writes, "all literatures were foreign. Trinidad was small, remote and unimportant, and we knew we could not hope to read in books of the life we saw about us. Books came from afar; they could offer only fantasy." Naipaul's reading of Dickens required a cultural translation: "Dickens's rain and drizzle I turned into tropical downpours; the snow and fog I accepted as conventions of books."

Yet, he only had the British novel as his model. It seemed impossible to him that the life he knew in Trinidad could ever be turned into fiction. "If landscapes do not start to be real until . . . they are written about, societies appear to be without shape and *embarrassing*. . . . It was equally embarrassing to attempt to write of what I saw. . . . Very little of what I read was of help. . . . The vision was alien; it diminished my own and did not give me the courage to do a simple thing like mentioning the name of a Port of Spain street."

When his father died in 1953, Naipaul did not return to Trinidad. His family was in distress, there were debts to pay, but Naipaul felt that he was in no position to be able to help anyone. He felt that he should have helped them, have gone back, but his sense of a vocation overruled his feelings: "Without having become a writer, I couldn't go back." His scholarship money, however, did allow him to return to Trinidad a few years later, in 1956. The island seemed to him to have shrunk and to hold no purpose for him. The only way that he felt he could look after himself was to be in England, where he could become a writer, an individual.

With his mind wandering between the rich cultural traditions of England and the seemingly hollow world of Trinidad, Naipaul attempted to find his place as a writer. After leaving Oxford he worked for a time in the BBC Caribbean Service, presenting a weekly literary program for the Caribbean. One afternoon in his office, "without having any idea of where I was going, and not perhaps intending to type to the end of the page, I wrote: *Every morning when he got up Hat would sit on the banister of his back verandah and shout across, 'What happening there, Bogart?'* " With that Port-of-Spain memory, when Naipaul was only twelve years old, with that sentence, Naipaul at last shaped the first words of his first book, *Miguel Street*. He had risked the embarrassment and began to make real for the first time the landscape of his past. After eleven months in London he wrote about Bogart: "I wrote my book; I wrote another. I began to go back."

At this point the details of Naipaul's private life become scant and he begins to incorporate his memories and feelings into his fiction and travel books where he parcels out his life among his numerous characters. Sometimes the parallels between his life and his fictional characters are obvious. Bogart and the other characters from *Miguel Street*, *The Mystic Masseur*, and *The Suffrage of Elvira* are based upon the people he came to know in Port of Spain and in the smaller towns of Trinidad. Mohun Biswas's search for a house in *A House for Mr. Biswas,* his battles with his wife's family, and his mental breakdown are all clearly modeled after Naipaul's father. Frequently, however, Naipaul's personal feelings and attitudes surface more subtly, sometimes from unlikely characters. For example, in *The Enigma of Arrival* Naipaul reveals that it was his temperament "to see the possibility, the certainty, of ruin, even at the moment of creation." In his novel *Guerrillas,* however, he transfers this obsession to the rather unpleasant character of Jane, a white Englishwoman: "She had always seen decay about her . . . and in the decor of a fashionable new restaurant, in the very newness, she could see hints of the failure and shoddiness to come."

In 1957 he published his first novel, *The Mystic Masseur,* followed the next year by *The Suffrage of Elvira.* He received the John Llewellyn Rhys Memorial Prize for *The Mystic Masseur,* which bolstered his self-confidence as a writer in an alien country. Since his books did not earn him much money, he served as fiction reviewer on the staff of *The New Statesman* until 1961. Although *Miguel Street* was the first book he wrote, he waited until 1959, after he had established a modest reputation as a novelist, to publish it. In 1961 the book was awarded the Somerset Maugham Award.

In 1960, on a scholarship granted by the government of Trinidad and Tobago, Naipaul returned to Trinidad for the second time. With the intervention of Premier Eric Williams, the time of the scholarship was extended so that Naipaul could write a nonfiction account of the West Indies. The book, finally published as *The Middle Passage* in 1962, presents Naipaul's impressions of Trinidad, British Guiana, Surinam, Martinique, and Jamaica. Naipaul's study demonstrates the enormous impact that slave labor had upon the formation of these former colonies. One of the major themes that Naipaul develops in the book derives from the depressing observation by James Anthony Froude, quoted in the book's epigraph, that "there are no people there in the true sense of the word, with a character and purpose of their own."

Naipaul's reputation as a novelist became more secure in England in 1961, with his publication of *A House for Mr. Biswas.* Reviewers and subsequent critics agreed that this long novel of a man's search for independence and dignity transcended the local color of Naipaul's earlier work and possessed a universal appeal of the first order.

The many strands of his family's history that he wove into this novel renewed Naipaul's interest in the mysterious world of his ancestors.

In an attempt to understand the mythical land of his grandfather, Naipaul began a yearlong tour of India in 1962. "In traveling to India," Naipaul writes, "I was traveling to an un-English fantasy, and a fantasy unknown to Indians of India: I was traveling to the peasant India that my Indian grandfathers had sought to recreate in Trinidad, the 'India' I had partly grown up in, the India that was like a loose end in my mind, where our past suddenly stopped." His highly critical account of India was published as *An Area of Darkness* in 1964. In 1977 he published a companion volume entitled *India: A Wounded Civilization.*

During his early years in England, Naipaul had convinced himself that he could never write about England. To him it was still an exotic world, fascinating but alien. With the publication of his next novel, *Mr. Stone and the Knights Companion* (1963), however, Naipaul achieved a personal tour de force in writing about an Englishman in England. Again, his newly adopted country responded with a distinguished literary award, the Hawthornden Prize. In 1967 he published another novel, *The Mimic Men,* and a collection of short fiction entitled *A Flag on the Island.* The novel earned him the W. H. Smith Prize.

In 1966 Naipaul began a lengthy study of the history of Trinidad. He was motivated by the same sense of being cut off from his past that led to his studies of India. *The Loss of El Dorado* (1969) focuses upon two central events in the history of Trinidad: the search in the sixteenth-century for El Dorado, the legendary golden city hidden in South America, and the British capture of Trinidad in 1797 and creation of a slave colony there. His exhaustive two-year study, based upon original documents, enabled him to see his homeland in a new light. He came to realize for the first time that the drabness and torpor he always took for granted as a child in Trinidad was man-made, that they had causes, that there had been other visions in the past, other landscapes. He tried hard now to look past the urban decay, through the plants and trees imported with the settlement and plantations, and past the depressing vision of Trinidad he had presented years earlier in *The Middle Passage* "to see the landscape I had created in my imagination . . . to look for the aboriginal, pre-Columbus island. I had to ignore almost everything that leapt out at the eye."

Having sold his house in England, when Naipaul returned there in 1970 from his travels in the Caribbean, the United States, and Victoria, British Columbia, he had to start life anew. From a rented flat in London to a house in Gloucester, he finally moved to a cottage in Wiltshire, part of an old manor near Salisbury and Stonehenge. He began writing *In a Free State* and during the nearly ten years that followed some of his best work flowed out of this peaceful, secluded valley.

Published in 1971, *In a Free State* was widely acclaimed as one of his greatest achievements in fiction. His reputation as a distinguished author, however, was still largely confined to England. With the publication of his novel *Guerrillas* in 1975 he became well-known in the United States. The title of the book, combined with its violence and sexuality, worked wonders across the Atlantic. Some discriminating reviewers, however, still favored his earlier work, especially *A House for Mr. Biswas* and *In a Free State*. In 1979 he published *A Bend in the River*, his second book set in Africa, that extended Naipaul's analysis of expatriatism and terror in a Third World country. In 1987 his autobiographical novel *The Enigma of Arrival* appeared and quickly became a best-seller in both England and America.

Over the years Naipaul wrote numerous essays and reviews for English and American periodicals and newspapers. Some of these pieces have been collected under the titles *The Overcrowded Barracoon* (1972) and *The Return of Eva Peron with the Killings in Trinidad* (1980). In 1978, when he was teaching at Wesleyan College in Connecticut, Naipaul was inspired by watching reports of the Iranian Revolution on television to investigate the Muslim mind. And so, the next year, he traveled to Iran, Pakistan, Malaysia, and Indonesia. In 1981 he published his findings in a book entitled *Among the Believers*, which he describes as a study of "a whole new generation of young people in remote countries, made restless and uncertain in the late-twentieth century . . . by the undoing of their old certainties, and looking for false consolation in the mind-quelling practices of a simple revealed religion." Then, in 1984, Naipaul published *Finding the Center*, consisting of two personal narratives: "Prologue to an Autobiography" and "The Crocodiles of Yamoussoukro."

Essentially one must seek Naipaul the man in Naipaul the writer. There is, however, one personal account of Naipaul when he came to the United States in the fall of 1978 to teach at Wesleyan University. One of his students there by the name of M. Banning Eyre, who became friendly with the writer, has written a remarkable essay about Naipaul at Wesleyan that presents a fascinating aspect of the man at that time.[7] The essay is brutally frank and convincingly honest in its affectionate and yet critical assessment of the famous author's presence in the small-college environment.

In his early days at Wesleyan Naipaul was a great success in the classroom. Students flocked to his course on alien cultures in great numbers to hear him expound upon the discovery and exploitation of new worlds. Iconoclastic, eloquent, he captivated the students and challenged their thinking. He also taught a writing class, although he believed that creative writing could not be taught. One day he asked a student if he felt that the course was a waste of time, to which the student replied, "It's not a waste of time as long as you don't listen to the teacher." Naipaul was overjoyed with this answer because it reinforced his own sense of the futility of teaching writing, and after that day the student became one of his favorites.

In his alien cultures class Naipaul spent two days tearing apart Isak Dinesen's *Out of Africa*. He condemned her for omitting from her book any discussion of the building of an empire, the taking of native lands, and the pacification of the Masai and the Kikuyu. The students' attempts to defend Dinesen were quickly put down. He also attacked Graham Greene and Ernest Hemingway for similarly failing to give an accurate image of Africa. He characterized them as among the last of the imperialist writers.

One day he turned his attack away from other writers upon the class itself. Many of the students failed to hand in their papers when they were due. Naipaul fell into a rage, pounded his fist on the table, and went on at length about honor, faith, trust, and being cheated. "It's like the governments of backwards nations where no one can be taken at their *[sic]* word," he said. In Naipaul's violent reaction in this situation he was apparently reaching back in memory not only to the cruel lies and propaganda within Third World countries but to the painful personal betrayals he had written about in his novels.

Naipaul grew bitter and depressed about his teaching. When he had first arrived in Middletown he felt that he had made a mistake and should have left. He quickly gained the reputation among the students and staff as an ogre, a sexist, a racist, and a snob. In the classroom he continued to criticize other writers, American barbarism, and the exploitation within Third World countries. When the students asked him what was the hope of the Third World, he replied that it did not lie in technology, but rather in the development of intelligence: "The highest expression is mind—to understand."

Naipaul has apparently felt for a long time that his books should sell better than they do and that he should be paid better for them than he is. In an interview conducted at Wesleyan by Bharati Mukherjee and Robert Boyers,[8] Naipaul complained that his books have not sold well in the United States, that some of them in the past have sold only six or seven hundred copies. He also complained that the college did not sell the *New York Review of Books,* a periodical that carried many of his essays. Attempting to turn the conversation to a more positive note, Boyers said, "Still, the experience of teaching bright students must have its pleasures." Never one to say the expected, Naipaul replied, "Are they bright students? I don't know. I think it's bad to be mixing all the time with inferior minds. It's very, very damaging. To be with the young folk, the unformed mind. I think it's damaging to one."[9]

After Naipaul returned from a teaching break in England, he told Eyre, the student who recorded his Wesleyan stay, that he had planned to fire his agent after twenty-eight years. Naipaul had received only twenty-five thousand dollars for the American rights to *A Bend in the River,* which he was certain would be a great success in the United States. Indeed, it did become a success, and Naipaul was elated, sensing that he was at the peak of his career.

Naipaul then grimly returned to the "nightmare" of the classroom. He was teaching a course in the Literature of Rebellion. Believing that the real subject of good fiction is a criticism of what goes on in society, he divided literature into two groups: fairy tales, which reflect a society so secure that there is no need to question its structure, and realistic literature, which always contains the idea of rebellion. This distinction goes a long way in explaining Naipaul's favorite authors, which include such names as Tolstoy, Conrad, Balzac, and James.

Toward the end of the term Naipaul gave the students in his Literature of Rebellion class a warning, a message that he has spent much of his life interpreting in his fiction and travel books: "Ask yourself if here at Wesleyan you are being broadened and given vision or if you are learning how to be a part of a tribe, to participate in rites, but lose the ability to see yourself."[10] Detachment, analysis, criticism, understanding—those are the tools of Naipaul's intellectual trade. He has been honored for his clear insights into other cultures, into the human psyche, and into the inevitable extinction that both threatens and enriches one's life. But as both his development as a writer and this glimpse of him as a man teaching at a small liberal arts college testify, Naipaul's quest to escape his backward past and attain membership in high civilization has deprived him of a sense of humor, the mark of a broad humanity and security possessed by such authors as Chaucer and Shakespeare. Naipaul follows in the more narrow and intense tradition of such authors as Joseph Conrad and Matthew Arnold. Like the latter, Naipaul views literature as a "criticism of life," a serious enterprise for serious people. The quaint comic characters from Miguel Street have become as dolls that Naipaul has put up in the closet.

As of this writing Naipaul has emerged from the meditative years in Wiltshire that produced *The Enigma of Arrival* to seek once again a critical understanding of a subculture. In 1987 he traveled throughout the American South taking notes for his forthcoming book *A Turn in the South*. The recent deaths of his sister in Trinidad and his younger brother, Shiva, also a novelist living in England, must certainly mark turning points in his life, reinforcing his own sense of mortality and dislocation. It will be interesting, then, to see how he embodies his own anxieties, anger, and alienation in this commentary upon the South.

2

The Comic Island

Miguel Street

Although *Miguel Street* was published in 1959, after *The Mystic Masseur* (1957) and *The Suffrage of Elvira* (1958), it was the first book Naipaul wrote. These three books represent Naipaul's comic vision of life in Trinidad, a wistful chronicle of the provincial rituals and absurdities of island life. Despite the narrators' satirical tone and the implicit poverty, ignorance, and suffering that lay in the background of the stories, these three works embody a powerful sense of lost innocence and youth. When the narrator of *Miguel Street,* for instance, reaches his eighteenth birthday, he suddenly discovers that the fascinating people around him, who he assumed would remain always the same, have lost their sparkle. In three years, he says, "I had grown up and looked critically at the people around me. I no longer wanted to be like Eddoes. He was so weak and thin, and I hadn't realized he was so small. Titus Hoyt was stupid and boring, and not funny at all. Everything had changed." After his street hero, Hat, is sent to jail for beating up his woman, the narrator confesses that "part of me had died."

The part that died, of course, is the childlike wonder and innocence of the narrator that dominate the tone and atmosphere of all three early works. Like his narrator, Naipaul himself comes to see the people around him with a more critical eye. He becomes progressively more serious, introspective, and detached in his subsequent novels and in his accounts of life in the Third World nations.

Miguel Street is a collection of character sketches of the inhabitants of Port of Spain's Miguel Street during the 1930s and 1940s. This bizarre and comic world of dreamers, bigamists, poets, pyrotechnicians, and pundits is affectionately recorded by the young unnamed narrator. Like Naipaul, the narrator comes to find Trinidad too confining, too stifling, and in the last chapter he escapes from the island by obtaining a scholarship to study in England. His chronicles of life on Miguel Street are written some years later and reflect his impeccable English, which contrasts with the colorful local speech of the islanders.

Naipaul's re-creation of the Trinidad idiom is central to the success of these early books. If the characters in *Miguel Street* spoke in the educated English of the narrator, the book would lose its wit, comedy, and uniqueness. The street idiom is direct, physical, metaphorical, energetic, and sometimes brutal. Adjectives frequently appear as verbs, verbs often fail to agree in number with their subjects, and sometimes their subjects are very abstract. When Mrs. Bhakcu asks her husband if he is all right after his car slips off the jack and falls on him, he replies, "How the hell I all right? You mean you so blind you ain't see the whole motor-car break up my arse?" When Hat comes and criticizes Mr. Bhakcu for tinkering with a new car, Mr. Bhakcu threatens, "The moment you get this car from off me, I going to break up you tail." Hearing this, Mrs. Bhakcu reprimands her husband: "Man, how you so advantageous? The man come round with his good good mind to help you and now you want to beat him up?"

The characters seem to take delight in their colorful language. Hat, for example, admires Laura not only because she had eight children by seven fathers but because "she like Shakespeare when it come to using words." Laura used to shout at her children: "Alwyn, you broad-mouth brute, come here," and "Gavin, if you don't come here this minute, I make you fart fire, you hear." These characters also seem to enjoy quoting passages from Calypso songs, which appear to comprise the island's national poetry. When Boyee sees that Eddoes's baby does not resemble him, he begins to whistle the calypso, "Chinese children calling me Daddy! / Oh God, somebody putting milk in my coffee." And one of Laura's husbands, Nathaniel, boasts that he keeps her under control by a "a good dose of blows" and proceeds to quote from a calypso song: "Every now and then just knock them down. / Every now and then just throw them down. / Black up their eye and bruise up their knee / And then they love you eternally."

The language of *Miguel Street* is so fundamental to its atmosphere, rhythm, and characters, that Naipaul later declared that the simple opening dialogue of this book created the world of the street and established the framework for the rest of the book. This dialogue marked the opening not only of the story but of Naipaul's writing career: "Every morning when he got up Hat would sit on the banister of his back verandah and shout across, 'What happening there, Bogart?' Bogart would turn in his bed and mumble softly, so that no one heard, 'What happening there, Hat?' " Naipaul was twenty-two years old, recently graduated from Oxford University and working for the BBC, when he wrote those opening sentences for his first publishable book. "That was a Port of Spain memory," he writes. "It seemed to come from far back, but it was only eleven or twelve years old."

Hat was a Port of Spain Indian who lived on the same street as the Naipaul family. Connected with Naipaul's mother's family, Bogart was a young man who lived in a separate one-room building at the back of the Naipauls' yard. The first sentence of the book, Naipaul says, was "true." "The second ," he goes on, "was invention." The two sentences together, however, had done something extraordinary to Naipaul: "Though they had left out everything—the setting, the historical time, the racial and social complexities of the people concerned—they had suggested it all; they had created the world of the street. And together, as sentences, words, they had set up a rhythm, a speed, which dictated all that was to follow."

Although there are many autobiographical elements in *Miguel Street*—the characters themselves being based upon people Naipaul knew as a boy growing up in Trinidad—Naipaul distances himself from the narrator in several respects. His narrator has no father or relatives and lives alone with his mother in a house on Miguel Street. Naipaul explains that in order to simplify his life he had to abolish the numerous members of his mother's extended family and make the narrator "more in tune with the life of the street than I had been."

The microcosm of Trinidad is Miguel Street. As Naipaul puts it, he tried "to establish the idea of the street as a kind of club," which had its own "city sense of drama." In the story Bogart seeks freedom. In real life, Naipaul explains, Bogart was trying to escape from his Hindu family conventions. Although he advertises himself as a tailor, he possesses no skill. Given the name Bogart by his street friends (after Humphrey Bogart, who was one of the most popular film heroes of the time) and invested with an aura of mystery by these same people, Bogart wins the admiration of the narrator for being "sensual, lazy, cool." He is finally done in by women. In Naipaul's analysis, Bogart had taken the easy way out: "He was that flabby, emasculated thing, a bigamist. So, looking only for freedom, the Bogart of my story ended up as a man on the run. It was only in the solitude of his servant room that he could be himself, at peace. It was only with the men and boys of the street that he could be a man."

Each of the seventeen sections of *Miguel Street* focuses upon a single character. The sections are linked together by the narrator's voice as well as by the reappearance of various characters from earlier chapters. One of the most prominent recurring characters is Hat, the streetwise commentator whose insights and seeming self-sufficiency make him a big brother, almost a father, to the nameless young narrator. It is only at the end of the book that the narrator discovers Hat's failings. The young man's disillusionment thereby coincides with the reader's sense of compassion for the fallen street hero.

Naipaul develops almost all of his characters by focusing upon one or two dominant traits. Bogart "was the most bored man I ever knew"; Popo the carpenter was always "making the thing without a name"; Big Foot, a bully, was "the biggest and the strongest man in the street"; Man-man was mad; B. Wordsworth was a poet working on "the greatest poem in the world"; Eddoes "was crazy about cleanliness"; Uncle Bhakcu "was very nearly a mechanical genius" who spent most of his time disassembling his car's engine; Bolo's whole philosophy was never to believe anything you read in the newspapers; Edward (Hat's brother) modeled his life after the Americans; and Hat enjoyed life better than anyone the narrator had ever known.

The first character in *Miguel Street* is Bogart. The narrator first sees him as bigger than life: "He did everything with a captivating languor. Even when he licked his thumb to deal out the cards there was a grace in it." Besides being one of the most popular men in the street, Bogart is also a man of mystery. Without saying a word to anyone he disappears for several months. When he returns he reveals that he has gone to British Guiana and become a cowboy and a smuggler. Then he began running "the best brothel" in Georgetown when the police arrested him. Not only do these experiences change Bogart but the people on Miguel Street begin to see him as someone to fear now. Then he disappears twice again, each time returning a bit fatter, more aggressive, and sounding more American. Finally Bogart is arrested and it is revealed that he is a bigamist. Hat comes up with the details of his two wives. His first wife being childless, Bogart deserted her to marry a girl he got pregnant in another town. When Eddoes asks Hat why Bogart left the second wife, Hat explains, "To be a man, among we men."

One of the recurrent themes in *Miguel Street* is the ideal of manliness. With the exception of Laura in "The Maternal Instinct," all of the character sketches in the book focus upon men. The women remain in the background, in their houses, while the men rule the street and seem to run the small world of Miguel Street. The male voice is the dominant one and throughout the stories there are several references to the importance of a man beating a woman in order to win her love and respect. This macho ritual is even enshrined in the lyrics of the calypso songs, such as the one previously quoted. In the sketch entitled "Love, Love, Love, Alone" (taken from a calypso song that explains why King Edward left the throne), the well-to-do Mrs. Christiani leaves her physician husband in order to live with a penniless sadistic drunkard who regularly beats her. Even Hat acknowledges that it "is a good thing for a man to beat his woman every now and then, but this man does do it like exercise, man."

Naipaul sets in motion an ironic countercurrent to this antifeminist theme. As John Thieme observes, "the dominant pattern of the stories is centered on an ironic exposure of the pretense of manliness."[1] Naipaul exposes Bogart's macho facade and reveals him as a "flabby, emasculated thing, a bigamist." Nathaniel, who quotes the calypso "Knock Them Down," turns out to be on the receiving end of the beatings. Big Foot, the most feared man on Miguel Street, becomes terrified that he is dying after he cuts his foot on a broken bottle. Only the narrator witnesses this private humiliation. Later, however, when Big Foot takes up boxing and loses his first fight, everybody laughs at him and he begins sobbing like a child.

The ritual of male posturing and aggressiveness is fundamental to life in Miguel Street (and reappears in various guises in several of Naipaul's later works). Popo, the carpenter who is building "the thing without a name," has no children and therefore allows his wife to go out and work. Because of this Hat says that "Popo is a man-woman. Not a proper man." Later, however, after Popo's wife runs off with another man and Popo begins drinking and fighting everyone around him, Hat reassesses him: "We was wrong about Popo. He is a man, like any of we."

The narrator has difficulty coping with the reality that continues to intrude upon the image of the macho hero. When Big Foot loses his fight, for example, the narrator reports that "all of us from Miguel Street laughed at Big Foot. All except me. For I knew how he felt although he was a big man and I was a boy." More devastating still, however, is the narrator's discovery that Hat has been imprisoned for beating his woman, that Hat even needed a woman like other men. About twice the narrator's age, Hat is described as resembling Rex Harrison. "He didn't appear to need anything else. He was self-sufficient, and I didn't believe he even needed women. . . . And then this thing happened. It broke up the Miguel Street Club, and Hat himself was never the same afterwards." Hat discovers that Dolly has run away, goes after her, finds her with another man, and nearly beats her to death. Thus Eve and the serpent enter the narrator's Garden of Eden revealing Hat to be a mere corruptible mortal, dependent upon women, and not the manly, handsome, and cool British Hollywood hero after all.

Thieme's contention that "The Maternal Instinct" illustrates what is latent throughout *Miguel Street*, namely, that the society is fundamentally matriarchal,[2] is more inferential than demonstrable. Nevertheless, this chapter on Laura, the legendary woman of Miguel Street who had eight children by seven different men, is an excellent example of Naipaul's distressing portrait of the devastated hopes of the island woman. Laura is a strong, domineering person who, in order to support herself and her numerous children, sells her sexual favors. Despite all of her hardships she manages to raise her children with a certain degree of authority and responsibility. All of the selfish men in her life have not managed to make her cynical or diminish her sense of humor. She is finally broken, however, by the powerful influence she unwittingly has upon one of her daughters. When her eldest daughter announces "I going to make a baby," Laura is devastated. The narrator describes the painful scene:

> She seemed to be crying all the cry she had saved up since she was born; all the cry she had tried to cover up with her laughter. I had heard people cry at funerals, but there is a lot of showing-off in their crying. Laura's crying that night was the most terrible thing I had heard. It made me feel that the world was a stupid, sad place, and I almost began crying with Laura.[3]

Naipaul seems to see Laura as the representative of all the island women, doomed to broken dreams, frustration, and hopelessness. Their poverty and dependency have the appalling quality of deadly genes passed down through the generations. Given woman's place in this oppressive society, the strength of her character, her maternal instinct, cruelly enslaves her and predestines her children to repeat her hapless life. After Laura's daughter brings home the new baby Laura's house becomes "a dead, silent house." Hat's final comment demonstrates the stoical wisdom necessary to survive in this society: "Life is helluva thing. You can see trouble coming and you can't do a damn thing to prevent it coming. You just got to sit and watch and wait." Laura's daughter commits suicide and Laura, when informed of this by the police, simply says, "It good. It good. It better that way."

Most of the characters in *Miguel Street* are eccentrics and one of them, Man-man, comes closest to being designated mad. The narrator, however, has the wisdom to observe that "I am not so sure now that he was mad." Man-man, first of all, does not look mad. He is fairly good-looking, does not stare at people, and makes reasonable replies to questions. One of the ways he makes money is to train his dog to defecate upon the clothes that people have put out to bleach. Everyone is willing to give him these clothes and he turns around and sells them. His dog then gets run over by a car and Man-man spends the next few days wandering about aimlessly.

One day he suddenly claims that after having a bath he has seen God. (The narrator mentions at this point that Ganesh Ramsumair, the pundit the reader has already met in *The Mystic Masseur*, has also seen God). Man-man proceeds to announce that he is the new messiah. Some men put up a cross, tie him to it, and he cries out for the onlookers to stone him. When the people begin hurling the stones in earnest, Man-man cries out (in contrast to his earlier prayer, "Father, forgive them. They ain't know what they doing"): "What the hell is this? What the hell you people think you doing? Look, get me down from this thing quick, let me down quick, and I go settle with that son of a bitch who pelt a stone at me." Not really that mad at all, Man-man nevertheless is taken away by the police and the authorities lock him away.

The people in *Miguel Street,* it turns out, are almost all actors. Man-man is too convincing for his own good. B. Wordsworth, on the other hand, is a fascinating character who has adopted the role of poet as his persona. He resembles Lewis Carroll's White Knight in his gentle madness, and the narrator admires him and his talent. B. Wordsworth one day knocks on the narrator's door and asks if he can watch the bees in his backyard. He explains that the "B" stands for "Black," and that "White Wordsworth was my brother." He and the narrator become good friends. Wordsworth tells him wonderful stories about young love and nature. "He did everything as though he were doing it for the first time in his life," the narrator observes. His energy and imagination make the dull island come alive. He even makes a simple visit to a restaurant seem exciting: "I think I will go and negotiate the purchase with that shop," he says. In short, "The world became a most exciting place."

Wordsworth also makes the future bright with his great plans. His chief goal is to write "the greatest poem in the world," a task that would take about twenty-two years to achieve, since he writes only one line a month. The world that Wordsworth makes sparkle for the young narrator then suddenly turns dark. The boy visits him and finds the poet lying in bed looking old and weak. Wordsworth tells the boy that the romantic stories he told him were all false and that all the talk about his writing the greatest poem in the world is not true either. The boy "left the house, and ran home crying, like a poet, for everything he saw." The following year he returns to the poet's neighborhood and finds his house gone: "It was just as if B. Wordsworth had never existed."

Throughout *Miguel Street* the narrator undergoes several such disillusionments. Reality continues to break in upon the intimate fantasy constructed among the members of the Miguel Street community. B. Wordsworth is an important person in the narrator's development, for he teaches him the value of language and fantasy. A seer and a writer can, in fact, make the world an exciting place. B. Wordsworth may have been a charlatan, but he invested the ordinary with a colorful vision. When the narrator, for example, asks him why he keeps his yard filled with bush, the poet tells him a tale about a young girl, a poet, who loved grass and flowers and trees. She tells her poet husband that she is expecting a baby poet. The girl, however, dies, along with her baby poet, and the husband, out of respect for his wife's love of the garden, never touches it again. Thus the high, wild growth. And so the narrator, unaware that his friend is simply too lazy to mow his grass, has Wordsworth's untidy plot transformed into a garden of romance and mystery. With the narrator's final disillusionment at the end of the book, however, he sees all too clearly that the Arcadian world of his youth has vanished as definitively as did B. Wordsworth's house and person.

Despite the disillusionments there are the continuous efforts of the community to enhance their dull lives with fantasy. Fantasy becomes the lifeblood of the island's underdogs. When Morgan, the pyrotechnician, has his house go up in flames along with his fireworks ("It was the most beautiful fire in Port of Spain since 1933," the narrator observes), he is charged with arson but is not prosecuted. The inhabitants of Miguel Street then speculate about his whereabouts: "They said Morgan went to Venezuela. They said he went mad. They said he became a jockey in Colombia. They said all sorts of things, but the people of Miguel Street were always romancers."

Even Miguel Street's half-baked intellectuals are romancers. His head filled with big words, snippets of self-taught Latin, and fragments of Trinidad history, Titus Hoyt, I. A. (Inter Arts), "was a natural guide, philosopher and friend to anyone who stopped to listen." Although lacking the rich imagination of B. Wordsworth, Titus Hoyt is similarly obsessed with the written word. He persuades the narrator to write a letter to the *Trinidad Guardian* because "only big big man does write to the *Guardian*." The substance of the letter explains how the narrator, lost in Port of Spain, was rescued by Titus Hoyt. Hoyt feeds the boy words like "peregrination" and "metropolis" in an effort to demonstrate an educated style of writing, but the letter is never published. Hoyt then attempts to further his own education by studying Latin and also dedicates himself to training the minds of several young men in Miguel Street.

It is at this point in the story that Naipaul obviously uses Hoyt as a spokesman for his attack upon the ignorance of his people about their own country. "Titus Hoyt said, 'You see, you people don't care about your country. How many of you know about Fort George? Not one of you here know about the place. But is history, man, your history, and you must learn about things like that.' " He explains to his unwilling charges that the fort was built during the time the French were planning to invade Trinidad. The narrator's response to this revelation captures the essence of Naipaul's keen awareness of the insularity, ignorance, and demeaning self-image of his people: "We had never realized that anyone considered us so important."

The final chapter, entitled "How I Left Miguel Street," reintroduces Ganesh Pundit. The narrator's mother decides that her son has become too wild and needs to leave the island. She takes him to Ganesh (who at this time is a minister in the government and running for the MBE) to see if he can arrange a scholarship for him in London. Ganesh explains that there is only one scholarship left, for pharmacy. Although the young man has absolutely no interest in this subject, Ganesh reminds him that in London he will be able to see snow, the Thames, and Parliament. So, the narrator agrees and his mother pays Ganesh the appropriate bribe.

On the day of his departure, the narrator, having said his goodbyes to his family, discovers that his plane will be delayed for several hours and so returns to Miguel Street. The first person he sees is Hat. "I was disappointed," he says, "Not only by Hat's cool reception. Disappointed because although I had been away, destined to be gone for good, everything was going on just as before, with nothing to indicate my absence." The realization that he is not a vital presence, that his absence whether through travel or death, really alters nothing, that life grinds on with no regard for his ego or his place in the grand club called Miguel Street comes as a shock to the narrator. Furthermore there is a sense of déjà vu in this episode because earlier he had the same realization about B. Wordsworth when he returned to his street years later and discovered that his house was gone and that "it was just as though B. Wordsworth had never existed."

As the years slip past, the narrator gradually sees the fiction that creates and sustains all of his romanticized characters and situations in his narrative. Hat is no more than a woman beater, Titus Hoyt a stupid bore, Bogart a shallow bigamist, and the narrator himself, perhaps a fool for not having seen this earlier. "I left them all," he says, "and walked briskly towards the aeroplane, not looking back, looking only at my shadow before me, a dancing dwarf on the tarmac." The narrator more than Miguel Street has changed and what he is leaving behind is a stunning city pastoral, the breeding ground for the great romancers who inhabit and shape the fiction. *Miguel Street,* then, contains both a young boy's version of street heroes drawn bigger than life and his subsequent awareness that he must not look back to his fictionalized childhood, that he must accept the new reality and follow his dancing shadow to the airplane, to London, to new reflections.

In a 1979 interview Naipaul expresses a dissatisfaction with his early work, claiming that it creates a fraudulent world: "Of course, when you're starting, you really have got to try to establish a world and it's much easier if you can even pretend that the tribal culture *is* a world, that the life of the street puts you in touch with the wider world. The early comedies make this pretense."[4] After writing *Mr. Stone and the Knights Companion,* however, Naipaul says: "Only after that did I really get going."

Naipaul's concern that the tribal culture of Trinidad that he depicts in *Miguel Street* is not really a world at all tells more about Naipaul than it does about the book. Having abandoned the simple human comedy of his native land depicted in his early works for the complex tragedies of his later novels set in England, Africa, and the revolution-torn Caribbean, Naipaul has become mistrustful of the comforting simplicity, vitality, and camaraderie of his city pastoral. True, life on Miguel Street may only seem to put one in touch with the wider world, but that never appears to be a central issue in the book. The very fact that in the last chapter the narrator manages to move away from Trinidad to the cultural mecca of London makes the point that despite the delightful play among the rich array of eccentric characters, and despite the reassuring rituals of tribal life in Miguel Street, there comes a time when a sensitive, imaginative, and intellectual young man must break away from his tight little island, its colorful dialect and cultural limitations or else remain forever a child.

Once Naipaul does acquire a taste of the wide world he can never again return home. In his history of Trinidad entitled *The Loss of El Dorado,* Naipaul makes this point quite clear: "The Garden of Eden [Trinidad] was dispeopled, abandoned, repeopled, neglected. The place where I was born had been made by more than four centuries of misuse." Not only has his pastoral world been despoiled by Europeans during previous centuries, but his own childhood sense of its innocence has been undermined by his later experiences in Europe.

In *The Middle Passage* (1962), Naipaul portrays Trinidad as a down-at-the-heels, cultureless, noisy, exploited, and imitative society. He characterizes his homeland as "unimportant, uncreative, cynical," and as a place where power is recognized but dignity is allowed no one. "Every person of eminence was held to be crooked and contemptible. We lived in a society which denied itself heroes." There are no scientists, engineers, explorers, soldiers, or poets, Naipaul observes. There is no community; rather, only a mixture of various races, religions, and cliques that haphazardly find themselves on the same island. "It was only our Britishness," he explains, "our belonging to the British Empire, which gave us any identity." The chief degrading fact, Naipaul argues, is that as a colonial society Trinidad never required efficiency or quality and because these things were not required they became undesirable.

In light of this critical attitude toward Trinidad it becomes easier to understand why Naipaul feels that there is something fraudulent about his early fiction since it does not assume the broad critical perspective he came to express in his later works. Still, one can understand Naipaul's rejection of his Garden of Eden without accepting his subsequent personal prejudice against the simple energy and design of a work like *Miguel Street.*

Tales from *A Flag on the Island*

Between 1950 and 1962 Naipaul wrote several short stories (most of which appeared in periodicals in England and America) that he later collected in the 1967 volume entitled *A Flag on the Island.* Given their early composition and their affinity in form and content with the sketches in *Miguel Street* and with his two subsequent novels set in Trinidad, I shall briefly discuss some of them here. The long title story, however, belongs to a later period and will be examined in chapter four.

Written from the first-person point of view, "The Mourners" (1950) is a slight piece that focuses upon the self-indulgent grief of a couple for their dead child, Ravi. The narrator, a boy named Romesh, visits his wealthy relatives and becomes an unwitting audience for their recollections of Ravi. Even though Romesh does not know the dead boy, when the boy's mother breaks down and cries he politely listens to her grieved account of her son. Occasionally she regains her composure and asks Romesh a perfunctory question about his forthcoming examinations at school. She proceeds to show Romesh a photograph album crammed full of pictures of Ravi and he turns the pages "with due lassitude." Romesh becomes restless and is ready to leave when Ravi's father arrives home to regale him with more memories of the deceased. Naipaul depicts the father's superficial grief through his cliches: "It makes you think, doesn't it? Makes you think about life. Here today. Gone tomorrow." The father does not have any real concern for Romesh, either. Abruptly shifting the topic from his son's death, he asks Romesh why he does not start giving lessons to children. "You could make money that way," he says. When Romesh replies that he has to study for his examinations, the father simply ignores his answer and asks if he has seen the pictures they took of Ravi. Unwilling to hurt the man's feelings, Romesh says no and is faced again with the prodigious photograph album.

This sketch captures the rather familiar gulf that separates youth and age, the living and the dead, and suggests the self-indulgent and superficial nature of the mourners. The parents of the dead boy are so absorbed with their memories that Romesh becomes a mere sounding board for their sorrow. They have no real concern for him, no place for him in their grief. Similarly, Romesh has little reason to care about Ravi or the parents' loss. Uppermost in his mind are his examinations, his passport to the future. Although the mutual isolation of the characters in this story is simple and matter-of-fact, Naipaul later develops the theme of isolation and alienation on a much grander scale in such works as *A House for Mr. Biswas* and *The Mimic Men.*

"My Aunt Gold Teeth" is a more vibrant story, resembling the tales in *Miguel Street* and recalling the characters in *The Mystic Masseur.* The narrator's aunt is called Gold Teeth because after she married, this lyrical eccentric had all of her perfectly good teeth replaced by gold ones. Although she and her family are orthodox Hindus, she persists in shopping around among other religions that seem to accommodate her desires. A simple woman, Gold Teeth knows only the rituals and taboos of her Hindu family and sees the rituals as a means of obtaining her wishes. She feels she has been cursed to have no children and seeks to overcome this curse through any ritual or prayer available to her. And so, she begins secretly to visit a Catholic church in another county. Before long, she acquires a crucifix and holy pictures. "The prayers she offered to these Christian things filled her with new hope and buoyancy. She became an addict of Christianity," the narrator observes.

When Gold Teeth's husband, Ramprasad, suddenly falls ill, she believes that her unorthodox religious behavior is to blame and not, as the doctor insists, diabetes. Although she uses the insulin that he prescribes, she also consults Ganesh Pundit, the faith healer. The same Ganesh from *The Mystic Masseur,* he tells her that seven spirits possess her husband and proceeds to go through a comforting ritual that promises to seal off the house from the tormenting spirits.

When Gold Teeth confides her secret practices to Ganesh, he cleverly assuages her anxiety. Naipaul gently satirizes the Trinidadian homegrown variety of Hinduism here when the narrator observes: "In his professional capacity Ganesh was consulted by people of many faiths, and with the license of the mystic he had exploited the commodiousness of Hinduism, and made room for all beliefs. In this way he had many clients, as he called them, many satisfied clients."

When Ramprasad's condition continues to worsen, Gold Teeth, a typical Indian daughter, brings him to her mother's home. He begins to improve but Gold Teeth suddenly realizes that this house has not been spirit-sealed. Too embarrassed to ask Ganesh to protect the house again, she decides to pray to Jesus in the Catholic church. The rest of the family tolerate her burning incense at home before the pictures of Krishna and Shiva and Jesus and Mary.

One day the family enters her room and finds her prostrate on the floor, chanting prayers to Mary and Rama and crying out that seven snakes are after her. Ramprasad dies the next morning and the narrator's grandmother tells Gold Teeth that her husband would still be alive if she had "not gone running after these Christian things." The narrator and his family "listened in astonishment and shame. We didn't know that a good Hindu, and a member of our family, could sink so low." That evening Gold Teeth destroys every remnant of Christianity in the house. The story ends with a delightful irony that brings the plot full circle. Gold Teeth's mother says to her, "You have only yourself to blame if you have no children now to look after you."

As he did with his eccentrics in *The Mystic Masseur* Naipaul quickly sketches his main character with a physical detail or two—her gold teeth and her fat body—and endows her with a ruling passion, in this case a blind faith in the powers of religious ritual. Although this is a light comic story that presents Gold Teeth as a lively and resourceful woman trying in her mad way to make the best of her limited world, it also reveals Naipaul's critical perception of orthodox Hinduism in the Third World. Later, in *A House for Mr. Biswas,* he develops his satire of Trinidadian Hinduism through his account of the Tulsi family. Despite their orthodox Hindu roots, the Tulsis keep pigs and send their children to Catholic schools. The breakdown of this orthodoxy provides a continuing source of sarcasm for Mr. Biswas to use against his wife's family.

"The Enemy" (1955) is an especially interesting story for it has ties both to *Miguel Street* and *A House for Mr. Biswas*. Both Hat and Mrs. Bhakcu put in brief appearances here, and the major portion of the story Naipaul later incorporates into the chapter entitled "Greenvale" in *A House for Mr. Biswas*.

The nameless narrator tells of his youthful conflict with his mother, who decides to leave her husband and take the boy with her to her mother's house. Lured by the prospect of having a whole box of crayons, the boy decides to stay with his father, a driver on a sugar estate in Cunupia. As in *A House for Mr. Biswas,* the father realizes that the laborers whom he oversees are prepared to kill him in retaliation for his authority over them. He and his boy move from the barracks into a small wooden house where they spend a night of terror. The potential for violence is evidenced in the death of their dog, Tarzan, who is found hacked to death on their doorstep. The dog bears the same name and fate in the novel. To while away the evening the father tutors his son in such subjects as religion and art, even as he does in the novel. Then a powerful storm comes up and the boy begins chanting prayers to Rama to secure their safety. Terrified both by the storm and the prospect of the laborers killing him, the father dies of fright.

Now subject to his mother's control, the narrator decides that she is his enemy, that if his father were alive she would be kinder to him. "She was someone from whom I was going to escape as soon as I grew big enough." In the meantime, he becomes caught up in the progress that invades Port of Spain, where he is now living. The Americans and the British begin programs of social development, one of the signs being the disappearance of the latrines. "I hated the latrines," the narrator says, "and I used to wonder about the sort of men who came with their lorries at night and carted away the filth; and there was always the horrible fear of falling into a pit." Naipaul's revulsion at fecal waste later surfaces in *A Wounded Civilization,* where he dutifully describes the Indians defecating along the roadsides, and again in *Guerrillas,* where the Englishwoman, Jane, is sodomized, hacked to death, and buried in a latrine pit. "The Enemy" ends with the narrator breaking his hand as he and Hat attempt to knock down the walls of a latrine. He passes out from the pain and his mother, filled with anxiety, begins weeping over him. The boy concludes by wishing he were a Hindu god who could have all two hundred of his arms broken just so that he could see his mother's tears again.

The image of a frightened, creative, and sensitive father is obviously of great importance to Naipaul, reflecting, as it does, the character of his own father. This story captures a scene of powerful intimacy between father and son that Naipaul re-created nearly verbatim in *A House for Mr. Biswas*. By shifting the point of view from first person to omniscient narrator in the novel, however, Naipaul was able to present a more analytical and less subjective analysis of that relationship. Furthermore, Mr. Biswas does not die of fright, but recovers and is a changed man after his night of terror. In "The Enemy" the focus is clearly upon the boy; in the novel Naipaul is concerned with the development of his hero. The short story being an early work, Naipaul more readily allows himself to identify with the youthful narrator, who is both intrigued and confused by his father's dynamic and neurotic character. In *A House for Mr. Biswas,* however, Naipaul rather self consciously underdevelops the character of Mr. Biswas's son, Anand, in order to distance himself from the dominant figure of his hero, thereby avoiding an overtly autobiographical and subjective portrait.

"The Raffle," "Greenie and Yellow," and "Perfect Tenants," all written in 1957, extend the range of Naipaul's scope. "The Raffle" is a trifling story about a Trinidad schoolboy who wins a problem goat. The next two stories, however, are both set in England, anticipating Naipaul's first novel set in that country, *Mr. Stone and the Knights Companion.* "Greenie and Yellow" tells the story of a lonely and childless Englishwoman, Mrs. Cooksey, who entertains herself by arranging love matches with her caged bird. Her interference, however, leads two birds to die and her original, lonely bird, to become sick and morose. "Perfect Tenants" depicts a slice of lower middle class suburban life and continues to feature Mrs. Cooksey, the landlady of a London tenement. The narrator records the rather mundane lives of some of the tenants and the growing concern of Mr. and Mrs. Cooksey that the Dakins are not the perfect tenants they appeared to be when they first moved in, being rather careless with the premises and threatening to disturb the Cookseys' cherished image of respectability. The Cookseys finally evict the Dakins, whose flat is taken over by a middle-aged woman with a dachshund named Nicky. The narrator ends his tale by noting that the new tenant's letters "were posted on from a ladies' club whose terrifying interiors I had often glimpsed from the top of a number sixteen bus."

In all three of these stories Naipaul manages to make the ordinary somewhat interesting, a technique that he would come to master in his subsequent novels. Rejecting the melodramatic and the sentimental aspects of life, he focuses deliberately and rather remotely upon ordinary people in order to reveal their quiet battles, fears, and aspirations. The danger in such an approach, however, is that such stories can become tedious and their characters unmemorable. Naipaul makes more effective use of his ordinary characters in the later novels where he allows powerful feelings and overwhelming terror gradually to unfold from their mundane lives and to devastate them.

The remaining four tales, originally published in the early 1960s, are all set in Trinidad: "The Heart" (1960), "A Christmas Story" (1962), "The Night Watchman's Occurrence Book" (1962), and "The Baker's Story" (1962). Although none of these tales is exceptional in its own right, together they reveal Naipaul's developing concern with such subjects as sadism, failure, hypocrisy, and racism.

"The Heart" is the simple story of a ten-year-old boy named Hari. An only child, Hari is pampered by his wealthy parents because of his weak heart. He does not participate in school athletics, is fat and out of shape, and unpopular among the other boys, who delight in bullying him. To make matters worse, as he goes to and from school he must pass a house with a yard containing fierce Alsatians that try to attack him through the fence. His fears are later brought to a climax when several Alsatians pursue him while he is riding along on his bicycle. This trauma causes him to spend a month in a nursing home and to drop out of school for the term. On his birthday his parents attempt to cheer him up by buying him a puppy.

The remainder of the story focuses upon Hari's attempt to resolve his cowardice and frustrations by punishing the puppy whenever it disobeys him. The small animal becomes the scapegoat for all of the bullying and fear that Hari has undergone in previous years. At last he has power and control over his blighted little world and he asserts it with calculated precision. When his father accidentally runs over the dog and kills it, Hari's eyes fill with tears. His mother seeing the boy's reaction says to her husband, "Go after him. His heart. His heart."

Robert Hamner concludes that "it is apparent that though the tears may stem from a species of love, the source is not altogether healthy or pure."[5] While it is true that Hari would on occasion withhold his affection from the dog in order to control its behavior, there is little in this story that suggests Naipaul's interest in any species of love whatsoever. Hari's tears come in consequence of his loss of a victim, a creature that he can manipulate with the same vicious disregard as the boys at school exhibit toward him. The story is about the ruthless and sadistic quest for power and it traces the need for that power to its psychological roots: fear, cowardice, and vengeance. The force that drives Hari to beat his puppy is the same that drives the hand that whips the children in "The Circus at Luxor" or compels Jimmy Ahmed to sodomize Jane in *Guerrillas*.

In "A Christmas Story" Naipaul turns his interest to the subject of a converted Hindu schoolmaster's dreadful sense of failure and paranoia. Having freed himself from the limitations placed upon him by his Hindu upbringing, the narrator feels that his lately acquired Presbyterianism opens the door for his success as a teacher in the Presbyterian schools. "Backwardness has always roused me to anger," he declares. For the sake of progress, however, he has deliberately cut himself off from his family and their outmoded traditions. The narrator thus reflects one of the many faces of Naipaul's recurrent figure of the alien or outcast. Suffering, however, seems to lie in the path of Naipaul's heroes whether they stick to their cultural lasts or rebel against them.

Fifty years old, the narrator carefully selects for his bride a woman some fifteen years younger than himself, a person well connected within the educational system of the island. They have a child with the solid British name of Winston, and the major difficulty that the narrator must face is his imminent retirement. Restless and despondent in his retirement, he suddenly is enlivened by the news that he has been appointed school manager, a post that promises to crown his otherwise successful life. Although he enjoys his new position of power and financial responsibility, he gradually becomes aware that he is incapable of managing the details of his grand project of constructing a new school building. Error after error, he continues blundering his way into debt and fears that his "entire career could be forgotten in the crowning failure."

Rather than face the possibility of being disgraced in the twilight years of his career as a capable Christian educator, the narrator plans to burn the new school down during Christmas. He even discloses his plan to his wife and child. Later, however, he has a change of heart and decides that he will not disgrace himself with an act of cowardice, that he will proclaim his failure to the whole world. His wife begs him to follow his initial plan and when he refuses, she leaves with Winston vowing never to see him again in hopes of disengaging themselves from his disgrace. Sitting alone, meditating on his fate, the narrator suddenly is visited by a boy who announces that the school is ablaze. "Even final expiation, final triumph, it seemed, was denied me," he reflects. His wife and child return and the family is happily reconciled: "So it was Christmas after all for us."

The fastidious, meticulous narrator, who breaks with his traditions and sets himself above his people, enjoys a paradoxical reward in this story. He maintains his dignity and carefully wrought reputation as an educator and administrator, but he knows he is a failure and has been denied the opportunity to be punished for his dishonest intentions. Instead of enjoying his retirement he finds his later years racked with paranoia, awaiting the Audit Department to prove him a fraud. The fact that the inspectors do not come after the fire means only that the world will not discover his family secret. The overriding sense of failure that dominates this story later resurfaces in such works as *A House for Mr. Biswas* and *The Mimic Men*. Naipaul's own insecurity as a young writer is reflected in his various personae as they struggle to find their place among shifting cultures.

"The Night Watchman's Occurrence Book" is notable chiefly for its unusual style. It is written as a diary of a night watchman who dutifully and naively records the comings and goings of various people at the hotel where he is employed. What he never understands is that the hotel is being used for prostitution and that the manager, to whom he is reporting, is involved in the proceedings. The night watchman's dialect adds to the humor of the piece. As he explains, "All I want is a little quiet night work and all I getting is abuse."

"The Baker's Story" is also a comic tale but one that focuses upon the racism in Trinidad. The narrator, a Grenadian, "Black as the Ace of Spades, and ugly to match," announces at the beginning of his story that he has become one of the richest men in Port of Spain. His account of his rise to wealth is a simple one. After spending years working for a Chinese baker, he decides to go into the business for himself. He quickly discovers that he cannot make a profit and cannot understand why. One day it suddenly dawns on him that "when black people in Trinidad go to a restaurant they don't like to see black people meddling with their food. And then I see that though Trinidad have every race and every colour, every race have to do special things." With that realization, he hires a boy who is half-black and half-Chinese to deal with his customers while he remains in the kitchen baking the bread. He concludes his tale with this striking observation about island capitalism and racism: "As I say, I only going in the shops from the back. But every Monday morning I walking brave brave to Marine Square and going in the bank, from the front."

All of these short stories, as well as the sketches in *Miguel Street,* exhibit Naipaul's ambiguous feelings about his native land. It is at times rich, colorful, comic, and innocent, and at other times it is stark, sad, oppressive, and degrading. Out of this swirl of Indians, blacks, Chinese, Hindus, and Moslems, out of the vertigo caused by poverty, ignorance, ambition, steel bands, and rumors of high culture in other lands, comes the developing world of a new writer who was to shape his fragmented creative insights into his first novel, *The Mystic Masseur.*

The Mystic Masseur

Many critics treat *The Mystic Masseur* as an apprentice novel, a stepping stone toward Naipaul's introspective, solemn, more self-conscious novels. Indeed, not only the critics but Naipaul himself seems to feel that his novels have improved from the early days. In a 1964 interview Naipaul describes *Miguel Street* as "a young man's book," written in the joy of discovering how to write without fumbling. He goes on to say that "*The Mystic Masseur* was written in the same sort of spirit, and then I wrote *The Suffrage of Elvira* to prove to myself that I could invent, invent a story constructed carefully round a given incident. Those three books were an apprenticeship, if you like, and then I was ready to write *Mr. Biswas.*"[6]

Such judgments exhibit what I would call the progressive fallacy. A writer might change his point of view, shift his subject matter around, develop a more polished style, or grow in wisdom, but his writing does not necessarily improve with age. Many examples could be cited to demonstrate this, but simply recall the lyrical beauty of Wordsworth's "Tintern Abbey," written in his youth, with the unpleasant didacticism of his sonnets on capital punishment, written in his old age. Or compare the dramatic intensity of Graham

Greene's early novels, such as *Brighton Rock* and *The Power and the Glory*, with his comparatively uninspired later productions like *Dr. Fischer of Geneva* and *Getting to Know the General.*

The Mystic Masseur is a comic masterpiece, much underrated by the critics. The novel is filled with characters who come alive, whose dialect speech gives a comic twist or poignancy to everything they say. Besides the array of colorful characters and sparkling dialogue, Naipaul manages to convey a sense of human compassion for his characters. The hero, Ganesh Ramsumair, exhibits a broad range of feeling and through his dynamic personality he brings life and drama to everyone around him. He is intelligent, resourceful, has a sense of the absurd and a lively imagination. And, like the hero of *Mr. Stone and the Knights Companion* and Ralph Singh of *The Mimic Men,* Ganesh is a writer. Although some readers see *The Mystic Masseur* simply as a parody of life in Trinidad, or as a cynical or contemptuous treatment of a land and people Naipaul abandoned for high culture, such views overlook the Dickensian richness of character and setting and the important theme of creative survival.

In one very telling sense this is a young man's book, as Naipaul said. The point of view is not handled very skillfully. The narrator is a Trinidadian who was treated by Pundit Ganesh when he was a small child. Years later, in 1954, when the narrator is completing his work at an English university, he meets Ganesh for a second time. Ganesh Ramsumair is now G. Ramsay Muir, diplomat (member of the Order of the British Empire). Although the narrator may have read Ganesh's books, he is in no position to be able to record the details of the pundit's life and the numerous dialogues that take place between the characters. In fact, the narrator calls attention to himself only three times: once at the beginning of the story, then briefly in the middle (when he gets to the point in his narrative where Ganesh becomes a mystic masseur and his mother brings him as a child to be healed), and again in the short epilogue. The story is essentially told from the point of view of an omniscient narrator. His observation that "the history of Ganesh is, in a way, the history of our times," may be an exaggeration but it contains a kernel of truth in its chronicling of Ganesh's rise from masseur to mystic to MBE. The history of the self-made man, from Samuel Smiles's *Self Help* to the Horatio Alger stories, has indeed been an alluring fable for the twentieth century.

The narrator quickly disposes of Ganesh's youth: he spent four years at the Queen's Royal College and then enrolled in the Government Training College for teachers in Port of Spain. His first teaching assignment is in a rowdy district in the capital. Over and over the headmaster instructs Ganesh in the purpose of the school: "to form, not to inform." Insulted by another teacher, Ganesh quits his job. He then receives a notice from someone named Ramlogan that there is bad news back home at Fourways. He returns to discover that his father has died. Happy to escape Port of Spain, Ganesh finds himself respected at home because of his education and his father's death.

Before long Ramlogan, the local shopkeeper, makes it clear that he wants his sixteen-year-old daughter, Leela, to marry Ganesh. Naipaul's characterization of Ramlogan is wonderfully drawn. A fat, almost black, man who seemed to have only one shirt open down his hairy chest to where his large round belly began, Ramlogan "looked of a piece with his shop. Ganesh got the impression that every morning someone went over everything in it—scales, Ramlogan, and all—with a greased rag."

While Ramlogan is manipulating events to marry off his daughter, Ganesh meets a man named Mr. Stewart, who has a decisive influence upon his life. Dressed as a Hindu mendicant and assumed to be from England, wealthy, and somewhat mad, Stewart captures Ganesh's imagination, serving as a model for Ganesh's later role as a Hindu mystic.

Keenly aware of the near magical power of education and writing to liberate one from the stifling culture of Trinidad, Naipaul delights in rendering both the naive worship of education by the uneducated islander as well as the wily manipulation of that learning by his hero. Ramlogan, for example, boasts to Ganesh that both his daughters can read and write. He shows Ganesh a sign that Leela made, which reads:

NOTICE!
NOTICE, IS. HEREBY; PROVIDED: THAT, SEATS!
ARE, PROVIDED, FOR; FEMALE: SHOP, ASSISTANTS!

Ganesh simply observes that "Leela know a lot of punctuation marks." But then it is Ramlogan's and Leela's turn to be impressed when Ganesh, arranging some booklets on the table, announces that "one day I go write books like these. Just like these." Leela's eyes grow wider and Ramlogan shakes his head in amazement. Ganesh's impulsive boast proves to be a self-fulfilling prophecy. What makes this boast seem so outrageous is the absence of a literary tradition in Trinidad. As Badseo, the young printer in the novel says, "You ever hear of Trinidad people writing books?"

Naipaul treats the subject of marriage in a very unromantic manner in most of his novels. Usually, a marriage simply happens and the couple grow accustomed to each other. One day Ramlogan tells Ganesh that he thinks it a good idea for him to marry Leela. Ganesh replies, "All right." And that's it.

Ganesh's wealthy aunt, called The Great Belcher because of her flatulence, arrives for the wedding with her friend King George, a tall and silent woman who helps manage the sundry affairs. When Ganesh learns that Ramlogan is charging the cost of all the food to him, Ganesh uses the ritual of eating the kedgeree for revenge. According to Indian custom the father of the bride must pay the groom to eat the kedgeree (a plate of rice and beans). Ganesh refuses to eat and the crowds jeer for Ramlogan to give more money. By the end of the ritual Ganesh obtains a cow and a heifer, fifteen hundred dollars in cash, a house in Fuente Grove, and the wrath of Ramlogan. He is now equipped to undertake his new career: "A little bit of massaging and a little bit of writing."

The tradition of wife beating that Naipaul refers to in this and later novels is one that is met with repugnance by many readers. Naipaul's satiric tone, however, suggests that these ritual beatings leave no marks, no scars, but serve as their initiation into adult society: "It was their first beating, a formal affair done without anger on Ganesh's part or resentment on Leela's; and although it formed no part of the marriage ceremony itself, it meant much to both of them. It meant that they had grown up and become independent."

Naipaul's memorable description of Fuente Grove not only roots the story in a realistic setting but serves to reinforce the theme of creativity. Through his creative and dynamic imagination Ganesh reshapes himself into a mystic masseur and turns the unknown, dreary wasteland around him into a famous center of healing, a place filled with excitement and drama. Fuente Grove was practically lost on most maps. In the dry season the earth was baked and cracked, and in the rainy season it turned to mud. The only tree in the village was Ganesh's mango. Once a year there was a harvest festival that "made a brave show of gaiety" but it "was like the gaiety of a starving child."

As the novel develops it becomes clear that the role of the women is a fixed and subservient one. The reader is told that Leela could have no children, that she became a good housekeeper, a ruler in the house, and that she and Ganesh "had grown to love each other." The women in Naipaul's later fiction do not fare so well, and the idea of mutual love between a man and a woman practically disappears from his mature work, with the exception of *Mr. Stone and the Knights Companion*. Where there is routine, old-fashioned traditions, appropriate subservience, and muted sexuality the women in Naipaul's fiction can happily coexist with their men.

Failing as a masseur (he offends his patients by telling them that there is nothing wrong with them) and having no children to father, Ganesh turns to writing: "Going to write a book. Big book," he announces to Leela. The narrator suggests that if he had become a successful masseur or the father of a large family, his hidden talents may never have flourished. Indeed, if Naipaul himself had been a contented family man working happily at some menial job in Trinidad, he might never have become a writer himself. The romantic notion that writing arises out of pain and serves to shape one's disordered life lies at the heart of both Ganesh's and Naipaul's vision.

Naipaul's parody of the worshipful attitude of the uneducated toward books is well executed in the scene with Ganesh and his friend and advisor, Beharry. Ganesh and Beharry are discussing a folder Beharry received from the Everyman Library:

> Ganesh said, "Nine hundred and thirty book at two shilling a book. Altogether that make—"
> "Four hundred and sixty dollars."
> "Is a lot of money."
> Beharry said, "Is a lot of book."

"If a man read all those book, it go have nobody at all to touch him in the line of education. Not even the Governor."[7]

Ganesh proceeds to buy only three hundred of the volumes and the post office delivers them in a van. It was one of the biggest things that had happened to Fuente Grove.

Ganesh's devotion to note taking, paper buying, paper smelling (he enjoys the rich and varied scents of different paper), and reading eventually drives Leela to run away to her family. She cannot tolerate their growing poverty, especially since her sister, married to a wealthy man, is doing so much better than she is. Naipaul undercuts the melodrama of Leela's leaving by the semiliterate note she leaves for Ganesh: *"I, cannot; live: here, and, put; up: with. the, insult; of: my. Family!"*

During the next five weeks Ganesh works industriously on his book. Naipaul captures the childlike innocence and excitement of Ganesh and Beharry as they discuss the incredible novelty of a book. All of the talk is about the paper, number of pages, binding, and other externals. Ganesh has a thousand copies printed and brings home his harvest in a taxi. He then goes to retrieve Leela and overwhelms her by producing the book he wrote in her absence. "Oh, man! Oh, man! Oh, man, you really write the book," she exclaims. "Careful! Don't touch it with your soapy hand," he replies.

The book temporarily brings about a harmony among Ganesh, Leela, and Ramlogan. The latter proudly reads the title of the new little volume: "A Hundred and One Questions and Answers on the Hindu Religion. . . . It sound nice, man. Eh, Leela?" Ramlogan repeats the title, shaking his head and smiling until tears come to his eyes. The following scene is a good example of how Naipaul embodies an affectionate attitude toward his childlike characters while simultaneously satirizing their ignorance and limitations:

> Ramlogan turned a few more pages and read aloud: "Question Number Forty-Six. Who is the greatest modern Hindu? Leela, just let me hear you answer that one."
>
> "Let me see now. Is—Mahatma Gandhi, eh?"
>
> "Right, girl. Fust class. Is the selfsame answer it have in the book. Is really a nice book, man, sahib. Full of nice little things to know."
>
> "Let me see now," Ramlogan continued. "Listen to this one, Leela. Question Number Forty-Seven. Who is the second greatest modern Hindu?"
>
> "I did know. But I forget now." (p. 101)

Despite the adulation of Beharry, Ramlogan, and Leela, Ganesh's book does not sell. Rather than being depressed with its failure, Ganesh turns his energy toward becoming a mystic. He and Beharry produce an advertisement that later becomes famous: WHO IS THIS GANESH? Unhappy to be called simply a pundit, Ganesh nails a signboard on his mango tree that reads: GANESH, *Mystic*. Following the colorful example of the mendicant Hindu, Mr. Stewart, Ganesh abandons his trousers and shirt for the proper dhoti and *koortah*. And he is in business.

From this point on Ganesh achieves one remarkable success after another. As a mystic masseur he cures the hallucinations of a small boy who fears a black cloud that follows and threatens to kill him. The boy, who feels guilty over his brother's death, is exorcised during a dramatic encounter between Ganesh (with the help of Leela, who chants in Hindi along with her husband) and the deadly cloud. Ganesh's success not only wins the gratitude of the boy's mother and Beharry's compliment—"You is the mystic massager"—but leads to a tremendous influx of patients from all over Trinidad. Fuente Grove is about to become famous.

Naipaul take pains to suggest that Ganesh is not simply a fraud. Rather, he is an ambiguous character, who cares about other people but at the same time is capable of trickery if it advances his and his client's cause. Of the boy being chased by the cloud, for example, Ganesh tells Leela that "this is the most important case anybody ever handle in the world. I know that boy going to dead tomorrow unless I do something for him." Ganesh is aware of the relationship between drama and reality: "Is like watching a theatre show and then finding out afterwards that they was really killing people on stage." Nevertheless, when he explains that the boy's mother saw one devil, the father forty devils, the boy one cloud, and Leela one cloud, Ganesh adds: "Girl, whatever Suruj Mooma [Beharry's wife] say about education, it have it uses sometimes." Leela is stunned by this and says, "Oh, man, don't tell me you use a trick on them," and the narrator simply adds, "Ganesh didn't say."

It is now to Naipaul's advantage to have a fellow islander as the narrator of his story. Though more sophisticated than Beharry and Ramlogan, the narrator has the same blind faith in education: "You never felt that he [Ganesh] was a fake and you couldn't deny his literacy or learning—not with all those books." His prestige and superiority are secured by his learning. Suddenly *101 Questions and Answers on the Hindu Religion* becomes the first best-seller in the history of Trinidad.

Ramlogan is also a resourceful man and acquires a monopoly on the taxi service bringing the hundreds of clients to Fuente Grove. Learning this, Ganesh outmaneuvers his father-in-law and forces him to sell the business to him, whereupon he quickly reduces the outrageous rates being charged the people. Over and again, the narrator makes clear that while Ganesh is amassing his fortune he never gouges his people. "But more than his powers, learning, or tolerance, people like his charity," the narrator tells us. Ramlogan's frustrated greed, however, leads him to initiate a series of attacks upon Ganesh in a newspaper run by a politician named Narayan. Ganesh eventually turns this fierce opposition to his own advantage.

As The Great Belcher points out, "Is the thing about Indians here. They hate to see another Indian get on." And get on Ganesh does. He prospers and so does his wife, Beharry, and all of Fuente Grove. Leela becomes more refined and begins buying expensive jewelry. "But the most important change," the reader is told, "was in her English. She used a private accent which softened all harsh vowel sounds; her grammar owed nothing to anybody, and included a highly personal conjugation of the verb to be." In the mimic world of Trinidad, whose models were the English and the Americans, especially the latter during the 1940s, the surest sign of social ascendancy is the spoken language. To sound like a Ramlogan is to be a Ramlogan. As Ganesh told Leela earlier in the story, "Is high time we realize that we living in a British country and I think we shouldn't be shame to talk the people language good."

A key passage in the novel comes when Narayan begins to heat up his attack upon Ganesh as an anti-Hindu, racist, and atheist. Ganesh asks Beharry what would Gandhi do in a situation like this and then answers his own question: "Write. That's what he would do. Write." Having discovered the power of the written word himself, Naipaul has made many of his fictional heroes writers. Ganesh, Mr. Stone, and Ralph Singh, to name just a few, all share Naipaul's discovery that "writing is magic." "You have to pretend to be writing a book," Naipaul continues, "until you discover who you are."[8]

Ganesh's second book is called *The Guide to Trinidad.* This seemingly irrelevant production proves to be politically astute, for Ganesh sends free copies to all American Army camps in Trinidad, to export and advertising agencies in America and Canada. Before long, American soldiers pour into Fuente Grove to visit the mystic visionary and to drink Beharry's rum and beer. Ganesh now would sit on a platform under a tasseled canopy surrounded by his books. He looked "the picture of authority and piety."

Along with Ganesh's international fame he achieves a political victory over Narayan. Through a series of complex strategies in the press and in public meetings, Ganesh and his organization defeat Narayan in his bid to be reelected president of the Hindu Association. From there Ganesh enters national politics and gets elected member of the Legislative Council (MLC). At that point the narrator again reflects upon the positive benefits that Ganesh has enjoyed from previous defeats, disappointments, and now, from political attack by Narayan. "Providence indeed seemed to have guided Ganesh." Although the narrator seems convinced that fate has predestined Ganesh to be a success in life, Naipaul strongly implies that it is Ganesh's inner resourcefulness, native intelligence, and combative spirit that really lie at the heart of his successful climb to power.

Ganesh's first experience as an MLC proves to be a humiliating one in which he suffers through a formal dinner feeling alien and uncomfortable. Determined to show the officious fools of government that they cannot mock him, Ganesh moves to Port of Spain, where he becomes a public figure of great importance. Before long he dominates the Legislative Council and becomes the most popular man in Trinidad. He is sent to Lake Success by the British government in 1950 to defend British colonial rule. Three years later he is made an MBE and changes his name from Ganesh Ramsumair to G. Ramsay Muir. At last he has arrived.

Like Graham Greene, whose comic novels are frequently ignored in favor of his serious works, Naipaul faces the same critical problem. Greene attempted to protect his reputation as a "serious" novelist by coining the phrase "entertainments" to describe his "lighter" pieces. Naipaul employs an even more effective tactic simply by abandoning comedy in his later works and by calling his first three novels "an apprenticeship." There appears to be a kind of puritanical sense of high seriousness at work here, both authors apparently enjoying their capturing the spectacle of human comedy but then later disallowing their comic productions into their literary canon. The critics are much to blame for this perversion, for in their endeavor to seek out high culture they sometimes ignore, attack, or patronize a serious writer's comic mode.

One reviewer described Naipaul's early novels as an example of his "looking down a long Oxford nose at the land of his birth."[9] Other critics dismiss these novels as simple farces. Naipaul overstates his case when he writes, in defense of these works, "The social comedies I write can be fully appreciated only by someone who knows the region I write about. Without that knowledge it is easy for my books to be dismissed as farces and my characters as eccentrics."[10] The reader no more needs to be familiar with Trinidad to appreciate these works than he needs to know London to value Dickens's novels. Both authors create unique, self-contained fictional worlds that only suggest their actual counterparts.

Nevertheless, some critics demand more of Naipaul than mere social comedy. Kerry McSweeney, who is enamored of the later novels, complains that the early works "are not diagnostic of the society they depict and do not have 'universal appeal' because they invite the reader to witness, not to participate."[11] McSweeney is merely repeating the language of Naipaul's own criticism (in *The Middle Passage*) of West Indian comedy. The assumptions behind this criticism are questionable. Must all novels examine the problems of the societies they depict? Is it the job of all novelists to be social critics? Later in his career Naipaul becomes very diagnostic indeed, leading him to write several nonfiction books about such complex, problem-ridden societies as India, Trinidad, British Guiana, and Jamaica. Indeed, Naipaul came to believe that significant fiction must deal with society. He once said that the artist, above all, is a kind of social historian: "Art domesticates. Societies don't truly exist until they have been written about."[12] *The Mystic Masseur,* like Naipaul's other comedies, is an attempt to validate the world in which he grew up. Naipaul's later clinical and analytical probing of his past certainly does not invalidate the more expressive and lyrical creations of his youth.

The Mystic Masseur is simply a social comedy, as Naipaul says, the irony of which is carefully controlled through the device of a sympathetic narrator with limited knowledge. As with most notable satires, this one focuses upon such human foibles as hypocrisy, ambition, greed, pretentiousness, and ignorance. The dialect and local color may define the story as Trinidadian, but the joys, sorrows, and absurdities of Ganesh's remarkable life are limited only by his human nature.

The Suffrage of Elvira

The Suffrage of Elvira is Naipaul's first novel to deal extensively with the politics of Trinidad. The story is set in 1950 during Trinidad's first election held under universal suffrage. Running as candidate for the Legislative Council in the small rural town of Elvira, Surujpat Harbans, a Hindu, sets out to win the confidence of the town's eight thousand voters. His potential constituency is comprised of four thousand Hindus, two thousand Negroes, one thousand Muslims, and one thousand Spaniards. It is clear from the outset that Harbans will probably win the election since he has the support of the two most powerful men in Elvira. Baksh, the leader of the Muslims, controls over one thousand votes. Chittaranjan, an influential Hindu, promises Harbans three thousand Hindu votes and one thousand Spanish votes. Nevertheless, Harbans's opponent, a Negro named Preacher, stands ready to give Harbans and his power brokers a run for their money.

Naipaul relates his story from the omniscient point of view, a perspective that allows him to capture the folly of this Third World microcosm attempting to deal with the novelty of democracy. The narrator's ironic tone is reflected concisely in his comment about Trinidad's newly acquired form of government: "Democracy had come to Elvira four years before, in 1946; but it had taken nearly everybody by surprise and it wasn't until 1950, a few months before the second general election under universal adult franchise, that people began to see the possibilities." The key word here is "possibilities," a wonderful understatement for such activities as bribery, chicanery, finagling, and treachery.

In *The Middle Passage,* Naipaul remarked that Trinidad always admired the " 'sharp character' who, like the sixteenth-century picaroon of Spanish literature, survives by his wits in a place where it is felt that all eminence is arrived at by crookedness." The focus of *The Suffrage of Elvira* is upon the absurdity that results when a society that cherishes the charlatan adopts the rituals of democracy. In 1950 a new breed of politicians arose who delighted in vans blaring slogans over loudspeakers, door-to-door stumping, intrigue, bribes, newspaper advertisements, and the rest of the machinery that goes into a mock-epic campaign battle. Writing about the 1946 election in *The Middle Passage,* Naipaul bitterly observes, "Then the bush lawyers and the village headmen came into their own, not only in the Indian areas but throughout the island. Then the loudspeaker van reminded people that they were of Aryan blood." "Then," Naipaul concludes, "the politician, soon to be rewarded by great wealth, bared his pale chest and shouted, 'I is a nigger too!' "

The novel opens with a description of Harbans's unlucky approach to Elvira. A poor driver, he nearly kills two white women (Jehovah's Witnesses) and a black mongrel bitch. Later in the story the two missionaries and the dog especially become important figures in the political campaign. Harbans, a wealthy Hindu who owns a transport service and a quarry, comes to town to meet with Baksh and Chittaranjan. Although Harbans is a central figure in the book, Naipaul seems much more interested in the characters that surround him.

Baksh, who has both money and political clout, throws himself enthusiastically into the campaign, promises the Muslim votes, and insists that Harbans hire his seventeen-year-old son, Foam, to be his campaign manager. Already agitated by the bad omens of the two women and the mongrel, Harbans is easily manipulated by Baksh into accepting his plans. Furthermore, Baksh points out that Preacher has a skillful campaign manager in a young Hindu named Lorkhoor. And so Harbans leaves with his new campaign manager to visit Chittaranjan.

Chittaranjan is "the most important person in Elvira" and lives in the biggest house in town. A goldsmith by profession, he is never seen working, for he always employed two other men to do the actual work. He not only controls the large Hindu vote but is influential among the Spaniards of Cordoba. Furthermore, the Negroes like him and the Muslims respect him. Chittaranjan himself respects

Harbans for his adventuresome spirit in this new democracy. The goldsmith tells him: "Way I see it is this. In Trinidad this democracy is a brand-new thing. We is still creeping. We is a creeping nation."

Chittaranjan, however, has two personal problems that dominate his thinking. First, he has a young daughter that he wants to have married to Harbans's son. Second, he has a shopkeeper neighbor named Ramlogan (Pundit Ganesh's father-in-law in *The Mystic Masseur*) with whom he is at perpetual war. Their personal animosities center upon the breadfruit tree that grows out of Ramlogan's yard and drops its heavy fruit on Chittaranjan's house and property. During his negotiations with Harbans, Chittaranjan is informed that one of Ramlogan's breadfruits has just broken a pane of glass in the house. Leaning over his veranda wall, he screams out, "One of these days I going to mash up your arse." After exchanging insults, Ramlogan reverts to his characteristic self pity. He begins weeping: "*I* don't control no votes, so nobody ain't want me."

A moment after his heated argument with Ramlogan, Chittaranjan calmly tells Harbans that he must open a rum account with Ramlogan, who runs the only rum shop in Elvira. Consequently, his liquor will be an important factor in winning votes. By the time Harbans leaves the goldsmith his head is teeming with bad omens: the white women, the black dog, the loudspeaker van, the salary for Foam, the rum account, and the treachery of Lorkhoor (a Hindu working for a Negro). Harbans therefore "saw defeat and humiliation everywhere."

When Foam was a student in the Elvira Government School he became a fierce rival of Lorkhoor. The new headmaster of the school at the time was a young Negro named Teacher Francis, renowned for his slick city clothes and his agnosticism. Lorkhoor and Teacher Francis remained close friends while Foam became more and more resentful of their good fortune. He was especially angry when Lorkhoor got a job advertising for a motion picture theater from a loudspeaker van. The present election, therefore, gives Foam the opportunity to seek revenge upon both Lorkhoor and Teacher Francis.

In his enthusiasm to humiliate his rivals, Foam begins painting the slogan VOTE HARBANS OR DIE ! all over the town. Lorkhoor, however, whitewashes some of the letters on these signs making them read --TE-----N---DIE. When Mrs. Baksh hears about the sign she becomes hysterical. Her husband tries to calm her, pointing out that there are only nine members in their family and that the sign has no significance. Her superstitious mentality, however, leads her to look down at her stomach and exclaim, "Oh, God, Baksh, how we know is only nine?"

Naipaul's parody of the island's political intrigue is heightened through the characters of Dhaniram ("the best known pundit in Elvira") and Mahadeo ("an out and out fool"), both of whom work for Harbans. Dhaniram is enamored of the form of the election. "Words like campaign, candidate, committee, constituency, legislative council, thrilled him especially." Dhaniram articulates the new democratic philosophy. Having been promised contracts for his tractor, he says, "Is not as though you giving things to we pussonal, Mr. Harbans. You must try and feel that you giving to the people. After all, is the meaning of this democracy." Toward the end of the novel, after votes are purchased with both money and rum, Dhaniram expresses his newfound respect for the citizens of his town: "The people of Elvira . . . have their little funny ways, but I could say one thing for them: you don't have to bribe them twice."

As Harbans and his enlisted cronies drink tea and ponder their course of action (a Caribbean mad tea party), they conclude that since Lorkhoor is getting Hindu votes for Preacher, they can get Negro votes for Harbans. They agree that when a Negro falls sick that their party will take him to a doctor and pay for the medicine. The only problem, as Chittaranjan points out, is that Negroes seem never to fall sick—"They just does drop down dead." Nevertheless, Mahadeo is assigned the task of making a list of all Negroes who are sick or "going to be dead," and of keeping an eye on Old Sebastian, "one Negro who look as though he might dead before elections."

Meanwhile, the Jehovah's Witnesses are out persuading the Spaniards not to get involved in earthly politics. The real farce of the novel, however, centers upon the appearance of a mangy, starved puppy at the Baksh household. Foam's brother, Herbert, finds the puppy, names him Tiger, and hides him outside the house. When Baksh comes home drunk that night he claims he saw a large dog downstairs. The next morning it has become small. A superstitious man, he concludes, "Is only one thing. Magic. *Obeah*. But who want to put anything on me?" For the next several chapters, Naipaul shows how Elvira's politics are shaped by superstition, magic rituals, and curses.

Before long an argument between Chittaranjan and Ramlogan leads to a falling out between Harbans and Baksh. In a heated exchange over one of Chittaranjan's chickens found dead in Ramlogan's yard, Ramlogan informs his neighbor that Foam has been chasing his daughter. Enraged by this, Chittaranjan confronts Baksh, the two argue, and Baksh withdraws from Harbans's campaign to become a candidate himself. Foam, meantime, retaliates against the Witnesses by placing five dead puppies in the sign of the cross, below which he writes AWAKE. Obeah has more power to persuade than does Christianity.

Naipaul's nominal hero, Harbans, continues to fade as the story develops. Throughout the narrative one is aware of his shifting moods, hears him punctuate his dialogue with "ooh's," but he remains a shadowy, undeveloped figure. His political action committee find him an embarrassment and "wished him out of the way." He is at best a pawn manipulated by the colorful figures around him. As the election day grows closer, Harbans's presence is further overshadowed by an event his committee has been waiting for—the death of a Negro.

Although Mahadeo faithfully dogs Old Sebastian's footsteps, it turns out that a Negro named Mr. Cuffy dies. Mr. Cuffy, who ran a shoe repair shop that he named The United African Pioneer Self-Help Society, was Preacher's most loyal supporter. Harbans's committee immediately sets up a much-publicized wake for Mr. Cuffy in order to win Negro votes. Baksh, meantime, comes to his senses and returns his support to Harbans. As the title of the last chapter ironically indicates, "Democracy takes root in Elvira."

Ever since the five hundred car parade held in 1946 by the Party for Progress and Unity, no election, whether for city council or local road board was considered complete without a motorcar parade. All of the principal characters of the story are collected for the final display of their political success. Foam's loudspeaker van plays the Richard Tauber record of the campaign song: "And oh, my darling, / Should we ever say goodbye, / I know we both should die, / My heart and I." The mock-epical quality of the parade reaches its crescendo when all of the commissioned taxi drivers revolt, demanding ten gallons of free gasoline. The spectacle continues into the final polling, with Baksh officially announcing the winner over the van's loudspeaker. Harbans has been elected to the Legislative Council. Foam goes up to Chittaranjan and says, "Well, Goldsmith, we do it. We win," to which the goldsmith simply replies, "What else you did expect?"

The novel might best have ended with Chittaranjan's cocky question, but Naipaul adds a final chapter in which he attempts to tidy up several loose ends. The epilogue attempts a comic denouement but actually adds little to the structure of the work or to any knowledge of the characters. Ramlogan had promised the committee of the winning candidate a case of whisky. The day of the formal presentation turns into chaos as each member of the committee argues before the gathered audience the proper disposition of the whisky. As the crowd laughs, boos, or cheers, even Tiger is brought back for a final bark. Harbans's last remark is simple and to the point: "Elvira, you is a bitch." By the end of the day his new Jaguar is set aflame. Lorkhoor successfully exploits these happenings by writing an article entitled "A Case of Whisky, the New Jaguar and the Suffrage of Elvira." His piece wins him a position on the *Trinidad Sentinel*. Harbans gets another Jaguar from his insurance company, refuses to allow his son to marry Nelly Chittaranjan, and life reverts to normal as democracy takes root in Elvira.

The fundamental comedy of this novel derives from the fact that none of the characters realizes how foolish he is. The cool, detached tone of the narrator sees to it that everyone comes under his ironic control. Sometimes, as when he describes Mrs. Baksh's attempt to remove the evil spirit that Herbert may have imbibed from the dog, his language suggests farce: "Mrs. Baksh took Herbert for a spiritual fumigation to a gentleman in Tamana." It is interesting to note, in this connection, that the entire incident with the dog and the town's fear of obeah may not be as farcical as an American or European audience might imagine.

There is this amazing story out of Naipaul's own past. In 1970 a *New York Times* writer named Israel Shenker sent to Naipaul a newspaper clipping dated 1933 with the following headlines: "REPORTER SACRIFICES GOAT TO MOLLIFY HINDU GODDESS / Writer

Kowtows to Kali to Escape Black Magic Death." It was the story of Naipaul's father, a newspaper reporter, who wrote a series of articles revealing that local Hindu farmers had defied government regulations for combating cattle diseases and had reverted to ancient rituals of the goddess Kali to eradicate the illness. Naipaul, Sr., was told that he would develop poisoning the next day and then die unless he offered a goat as sacrifice to the goddess. He proceeded to make the sacrifice. Upon receiving this clipping, Naipaul was staggered. He recalled that his father had a special horror of the Kali cult, but refused to credit the story as anything but a bad joke. Two years later, when he visited Trinidad, however, Naipaul researched the story further and came to the conclusion that the story was not only true but "it was a bigger story than I had imagined, and it was not comic at all. It was the story of great humiliation." One wonders if Naipaul could have developed the Baksh family's comic fears over the dog and its black-magical powers had he known about his father's similar fears of obeah. The story, as the newspaper headlines clearly indicate, has all the necessary features of comedy and farce.

Naipaul presents two rather distinct views of Trinidad: the bitterly cynical and analytical one expressed in *The Middle Passage* and in other nonfictional pieces, and the satirical one embodied in his early novels. Naipaul's attitude toward the report of his father's sacrifice of the goat is a good example of this duality. What he says about the story concerning his father, his nonfiction says about the history of Trinidad: "It was not comic at all. . . . It was the story of great humiliation." And yet, when he was young, Naipaul was able to deal with his island world with the distancing techniques of satire, irony, and farce.

There are some critics, however, such as George Lamming, A. C. Derrick, and Peter Nazareth who are intolerant of Naipaul's comic mode and find his early novels to be patronizing, cynical, and dehumanizing. Nazareth says that *The Suffrage of Elvira* "is a sustained exercise in contempt for the people." He points out that the character of Ramlogan is made repulsive by the repetition of the word "greasy" and the details of his fat arms and scowling face. When Harbans says, "People should be uniting these days, man," Nazareth contends that "Naipaul shows his contempt for any attempt at serious comment by Harbans by adding the word 'man' at the end." All of the political comments in this novel, he argues, are cynical. He concludes that "Naipaul shows little understanding in this novel of political issues. Politics is merely a contemptible activity engaged in by contemptible individuals from and in a contemptible society."[13]

Nazareth's hostility is that of the humorless, militant leftist who would prescribe a more serious and sympathetic portrait of a Third World nation than he finds in Naipaul. He argues that English critics admire each and every novel by Naipaul because he presents "West Indians not as people but as things, thus creating *sophisticated* pieces of exotica for the West, but exotica all the same."[14] His most damning comment, however, is that Naipaul shows no respect for life in his novels and that without that respect a work of art cannot be created.

It might be more reasonable to argue, at least from the young Naipaul's point of view, that Trinidad afforded precious little life for its inhabitants. In order to gain a sense of self-respect and an understanding of his country, he had to leave it and take its measure from a distant perspective. Indeed, he fails to invest any of his early characters with a fundamental goodness and depth of feeling. From Bogart to Harbans, from Hat to Baksh, Naipaul's characters are morally neutral—incapable of great evil or great good because they live on a plain where cleverness, agility, appearance, stupidity, wit, and conniving seem sufficient to keep them going. If, as Naipaul says, Trinidad is a society that admires the picaroon, then his first three novels have enshrined that sharp character as the country's mock hero. The world of those novels, then, takes on the atmosphere of a comedy of manners in which style and wit and maneuvers displace such traits as good and evil and destiny. Despite the comedy of *The Suffrage of Elvira* the reader is left with a sense of the profound pettiness and emptiness of its characters, a hollowness that does not suggest a disrespect for life but rather a desperate attempt to make a miserably circumscribed life both colorful and energetic.

Naipaul's development as a writer from this point in his career is very interesting. Life suddenly becomes a serious affair for his characters. Subjects such as death, fear, sexuality, failure, and identity begin to obsess his heroes. The simplicity of life on Miguel Street, the excitement that Pundit Ganesh brings to Fuente Grove, and the childlike joy and energy that characters such as Chittaranjan, Baksh, and Foam put into the game of politics are aspects of Naipaul's past vision that dim significantly in *A House for Mr. Biswas* and then vanish completely from the subsequent novels. His last novel to be set in Trinidad until *Guerrillas* (1975), which is set on an unnamed Caribbean island, *A House for Mr. Biswas* (1961) is Naipaul's elaborate bridge between two worlds, one dying and the other powerless to be born.

3

Breaking Away

A House for Mr. Biswas

Naipaul describes *A House for Mr. Biswas* as the one book of all he wrote as the closest to him. "It is the most personal," he writes, "created out of what I saw and felt as a child. It also contains, I believe, some of my funniest writing." Most personal, however, are the fear and terror that underlie the entire novel. Having left Oxford to make his mark as a writer in London, Naipaul experienced an overpowering sense of failure and hollowness that he later incorporated in the sinews of this novel: "to have found no talent, to have written no book, to be null and unprotected in the busy world. It is that anxiety—the fear of destitution in all its forms, the vision of the abyss—that lies below the comedy of the present book." Naipaul's profound insecurity and his failure to realize a cultural sense of place crystallize into the dominant theme of this novel. He describes the book simply as "the story of a man's search for a house and all that the possession of one's own house implies."

Naipaul opens his novel where the story ends, with the death of his hero: "Ten weeks before he died, Mr. Mohun Biswas, a journalist of Sikkim Street, St. James, Port of Spain, was sacked." Forty-six years old, the father of four children, penniless, and owing three thousand dollars on the house he has been seeking all his life, Mr. Biswas is introduced to the reader as a seeming failure. The novel goes on to demonstrate, however, that while Mr. Biswas is as flawed as the many characters around him whom he constantly vilifies, he possesses a remarkable resilience of spirit that enables him to endure seemingly overwhelming hardships and torments. As a young man he read and admired the writings of the Victorian writer Samuel Smiles, an author who preached the gospel of self-help and told of amazing success stories of those who persevered in the face of adversity. Driven by romantic dreams he can never fulfill, Mohun Biswas nevertheless proves to be heroic in his struggle to assert his independence in a world that constantly threatens to devour his individuality.

The opening chapter also makes it clear that Mr. Biswas never enjoyed a house of his own from the time of his childhood: "As a boy he had moved from one house of strangers to another; and since his marriage he felt he had lived nowhere but in the houses of the Tulsis, at Hanuman House in Arwacas, in the decaying wooden house at Shorthills, in the clumsy concrete house in Port of Spain." In his last years, however, he acquired a house of his own, "on his own half-lot of land, his own portion of earth." Mr. Biswas's quest for a house becomes a quest for wholeness, identity, and independence. The search gives his otherwise absurd life a purpose and direction and comes to fulfill his sense of his own dignified humanity. Thus Naipaul can write:

> How terrible it would have been at this time, to be without it: to have died among the Tulsis, amid the squalor of that large, disintegrating and indifferent family; to have left Shama [his wife] and the children among them, in one room; worse, to have lived without even attempting to lay claim to one's portion of the earth; to have lived and died as one had been born, unnecessary and unaccommodated.[1]

When Mr. Biswas (as Naipaul calls him even as a child) is born a local pundit visits the house and makes some foreboding prophecies based upon his astrological almanac. Seeing the baby has six fingers on one hand, the pundit advises that the boy be kept away from rivers and ponds. By the time he is nine days old the sixth finger of misfortune falls off but Mr. Biswas does not receive a new lease on fate. As he grows older the malnourished boy discovers the joy of wading in a stream, something strictly forbidden by the pundit, and one day he leaves the family calf unattended and it drowns in the pond. When his father discovers what happened he dives into the pond in order to retrieve the body but drowns in the process. The pundit's almanac proves accurate, and Mr. Biswas, the unwitting cause of two deaths, is sent off to live with relatives. "For the next thirty-five years," Naipaul writes, "he was to be a wanderer with no place he could call his own, with no family except that which he was to attempt to create out of the engulfing world of the Tulsis."

For the next six years Mr. Biswas attends the Canadian Mission School at Pagotes. His mother's sister, Tara, and her husband, Ajodha, a wealthy Brahmin couple, live at Pagotes and exhibit a style of life that dramatically contrasts with that of his mother living in a mud hut in the back road. Most of the people living in the hut are strangers to him and he feels that his mother is too shy to show him any affection in the presence of these other people. Later, in the house of his mother-in-law, Hanuman House, this sense of alienation develops into an obsession. In Tara's house, on the other hand, he enjoys a brief fantasy of self importance, for there he is respected and pampered as a Brahmin. It is only the religious ceremonies, however, that provide a sense of belonging, for as soon as they are over "he became once more only a labourer's child."

Having worked unsuccessfully at several jobs, Mr. Biswas finally discovers he has an artistic ability and becomes a sign painter. Between assignments he begins reading such British authors as Hall Caine and Marie Corelli, who inspire romantic visions in him with their intoxicating descriptions of exotic (English) landscapes and cold weather. He also begins reading the writings of Samuel Smiles, finding him "as romantic and satisfying as any novelist." Mr. Biswas sees himself in many of Smiles's heroes: "he was young, he was poor, and he fancied he was struggling." Although Naipaul belongs to the school of realistic novelists, he portrays his young hero as one filled with dreams that eventually will be tempered with the crushing realities that lie ahead. Meanwhile, heading for a fall, Mr. Biswas "had begun to wait, not only for love, but for the world to yield its sweetness and romance. . . . And it was in this mood of expectation that he went to Hanuman House at Arwacas, and saw Shama." The rich melancholy of the novel derives from the complex web of the narrative. Like some spider-god, Naipaul lures his hero-victim into the web through the character of young Shama. Throughout the rest of the novel Mr. Biswas attempts to extricate himself from the circumstances he falls into and helps create, but he remains inextricably entangled. It is his heroic struggle to free himself from his entrapment that wins our attention and admiration.

Kenneth Ramchand views Mr. Biswas's struggle as a reflection of Naipaul's profound concern with West Indian rootlessness: "Mr. Biswas is an Indian who marries into an Indian enclave in Trinidad between the wars: he recognizes the blinkered insulation of this world from the outside, and he senses its imminent dissolution." On the other hand, he has nowhere yet to turn. He spends most of his life trying to escape his cultural insularity "only to find that the future, the colonial society upon which he wishes to make his mark, is as yet uncreated. Mr. Biswas struggles between the tepid chaos of a decaying culture and the void of a colonial society."[2]

Naipaul's description of the architecture of Hanuman House foreshadows the important events that come to take place within its walls. It stood "like an alien white fortress," its concrete walls are thick, its doors are narrow, its side walls are windowless, and its general aspect is "bulky, impregnable, and blank." The Tulsi family, who own the house, is a conservative, landowning family of pious Hindus. Pundit Tulsi, the founder of the family, was the first to be killed in a motorcar accident. He left the fortune he made in Trinidad to his wife, who, with the help of her brother-in-law, a powerful man named Seth, rules over the extended family living in Hanuman House, oversees other property, and runs the Tulsi Store on the ground floor of the family house. This domineering matriarch and her unruly household stand ready to swallow up the dreams and individuality of the young, hopeful sign painter employed to create signs for the Tulsi Store.

Mr. Biswas becomes infatuated with Mrs. Tulsi's daughter, Shama, and makes the mistake of writing a note declaring his love for her. The Tulsis intercept the note and before he knows it, Mrs. Tulsi and Seth manipulate Mr. Biswas into marrying Shama. He begins to feel at Hanuman House the same way he did earlier in his mother's mud hut: "In the press of daughters, sons-in-law and children, he began to feel lost, unimportant and even frightened. No one particularly noticed him." His great expectations of love, sweetness, and romance are quickly stifled by forces seemingly out of his control. His marriage to Shama is recorded in a brief paragraph that describes the ceremony as "make-believe as a child's game, with paper flowers in dissimilar vases on a straw-coloured, official-looking desk." Not only does Mr. Biswas not have a house of his own (he has no money and little prospects for independence), he feels trapped within this alien white structure. After getting married, the reader learns, "He spent the rest of that day imprisoned where he was, listening to the noises of the house." Naipaul expects the reader to understand that another dimension of Mr. Biswas's entrapment and humiliation lies in the fact that Hindu custom would have the bride live with the husband's family where she would become almost a servant to her mother-in-law. It is Mr. Biswas, however, who finds himself under the rule of his mother-in-law, a rule made even more difficult to endure since it is enforced by Mrs. Tulsi's arrogant brother-in-law, Seth. Were it not for the failure to heed the pundit as a child, perhaps Mr. Biswas's father would still be alive and his family kept intact. His sad astrology destines him to do battle with a powerful woman and her influential family if he is to salvage his manhood and his integrity.

Life in the Tulsi house is well organized. The daughters and their children keep the house clean, cook, and serve in the store. The men, under Seth's supervision, work the land, take care of the animals, and also serve in the store. For their services, their children are taken care of, they are paid small sums, and they are treated with respect by people outside because they are connected with the Tulsi family. As Mr. Biswas quickly discovers, the price they and he pay for such an accommodation is the loss of identity: "Their names were forgotten; they became Tulsis." Throughout the novel Naipaul reinforces this sense of lost identity by having Mr. Biswas categorize the family with comic epithets.

Rather than become a Tulsi, Mr. Biswas rebels. His lack of money and position, however, keeps him dependent upon Shama's family, and in his frustration and anger he packs up and returns to Pagotes. Knowing he has been irrevocably trapped by his precipitous marriage, he soon returns and resorts to sarcasm and irony to protect himself from the Tulsis. He begins labeling people: Shama's brothers become "the little gods" and "the monkeys," Seth "the Big Boss" and "the bull," and Mrs. Tulsi "the old queen," "the hen," and "the cow." "The place is like a blasted zoo," he exclaims to his wife. By his linguistic reduction of the Tulsis to the level of animals, Mr. Biswas maintains the illusion of control over an environment that clearly controls him. He also rejoices in labeling the family with generic terms, thereby suggesting their lack of identity. He speaks frequently of "the sisters," "the widows," and "the readers and learners." Recognizing Mr. Biswas's false bravado, Seth in turn says to him, "You want to paddle your own canoe. . . . Biswas the paddler." Unlike Mr. Biswas, Seth does indeed possess power, independence, and respect within the family and his assessment of Mr. Biswas is painfully perceptive.

Mr. Biswas next attempts to isolate himself from the influence of the Tulsis by attacking their religion. He notes that the family has compromised its Hinduism by sending Shama's two brothers to a Roman Catholic college. When the family speaks to him in Hindi he responds in English. Always on the attack, he one day has a sudden insight into the meaninglessness of his aggression. His campaign no longer gives him pleasure but appears degrading and pointless. He begins to think of the many houses he has lived in "and how easy it was to think of those houses without him!" Beneath all of his banter, anger, and frustration he recognizes the void that threatens to annihilate him. He has no house of his own, no independence, no respect, and no prospects for the future. In short, he has done nothing significant with his life. As Naipaul says, "There was nothing to speak of him." Hanuman House at least provides him some structure and a standard against which to rebel.

Seth is correct in observing that Mr. Biswas wants to paddle his own canoe. Both in Hanuman House and throughout the novel Mr. Biswas constantly fights to assert his individuality. His combat, however, is hardly heroic and often reveals him to be petty, mean, and contemptible. Nevertheless, as Gordon Rohelhr points out, "part of the book's triumph is that Naipaul has been able to present a hero in all his littleness, and still preserve a sense of the man's inner dignity."[3]

Mr. Biswas's days at Hanuman House abruptly come to an end after he spits on Owad, one of Shama's brothers, and Govind, the boy's uncle, attacks Mr. Biswas. The next day Seth summons Mr. Biswas to announce that he wants him to leave the house. "This was a nice united family before you come," he tells him, and moves Mr. Biswas and Shama (now pregnant) off to the Chase to run a small food shop there owned by the Tulsis. The Chase is a settlement of mud huts in the sugarcane area and its poverty and ugliness recall the home of Mr. Biswas's mother and the humiliation he always felt when visiting her there. Once again he has a "house" but not a home. At the back of the shop there were two rooms with unplastered mud walls and a thatch roof. Standing in this miserable, lonely, and frightening place Shama cries out, "*This* is what you want to paddle your own canoe with."

In order to endure life in his new surroundings, Mr. Biswas convinces himself that the Chase "was a pause, a preparation" and not real life, a notion that anticipates Ralph Singh's feeling in *The Mimic Men* that part of his life was lived within parentheses. In any event, Mr. Biswas was now free of the Tulsis, at least for a few days. Before long Shama begins to nag her husband to allow her family to visit for the blessing of the shop. When the family arrives they bring with them all of the tension of Hanuman House. Although the thought crosses his mind to leave Shama and forget the Tulsis, he realizes that his prospects are limited to his becoming a laborer or a shopkeeper. "Would Samuel Smiles have seen more than that?" he wonders.

When Shama gives birth to a baby girl her family chooses its name—Savi—thereby once again reducing Mr. Biswas's sense of control over his own family, his own destiny. He is further humiliated by discovering that the family has listed his occupation on the birth certificate as "Labourer." He takes the certificate from Shama and scribbles "Proprietor" in its place. In order to seek revenge, he informs a journalist named Misir that the Tulsis own a pig with two heads. Hindus, of course, are not supposed to keep pigs no matter how many heads they may have, but Mr. Biswas's anger at being labeled a "Labourer" drives him to this absurd retaliation.

Despite Shama's help in keeping the shop's books, Mr. Biswas manages to drag the family into debt through his blind trust in legal justice. He hires a lawyer who promises to secure payment for outstanding bills from one of the shop's customers. Mr. Biswas finds himself the victim of a scam when the accused man himself hires a lawyer (in cahoots with Mr. Biswas's attorney) who countersues Mr. Biswas and wins the judgment.

Mr. Biswas's romantic longings—his dreams of self-respect and of discovering some significance to his otherwise absurd life—are seriously trimmed during his six years at the Chase. A sense of boredom and hopelessness begins to overcome him. Significantly, he abandons his reading of Samuel Smiles (whose work he reads as romance novels) and turns instead to the stoical writings of Epictetus and Marcus Aurelius as more befitting his narrowing prospects. But Mr. Biswas's stoicism is one of imposition rather than choice. He still seeks bright avenues of escape from his barren world and begins covering the shop doors and the front of the counter with landscapes: "He painted cool, ordered forest scenes, with gracefully curving grass, cultivated trees ringed with friendly serpents, and floors bright with perfect flowers; not the rotting, mosquito-infested jungle he could find within an hour's walk." He also begins reading innumerable novels and even attempts to write himself. It is, in fact, this powerful romantic strain within him, like some primeval force, that drives him forward throughout the novel. Combined with an incredible resiliency of spirit, which enables him to survive both inner and outer battles, this dream vision of a better world, one that *he* shapes and orders, lies at the center of his being. The little paddler is a sort of diminutive Don Quixote locked within the text of a realistic novel.

Life at the Chase, meanwhile, grinds to a close. Shama has another child, a son named Anand. Mr. Biswas begins to recognize the value Hanuman House holds for him: "Though Hanuman House had at first seemed chaotic it was not long before Mr. Biswas had seen that in reality it was ordered." The word "order" has enormous significance to Naipaul's characters who are seeking identity and peace. Whether through writing, painting, or living within a highly structured family, one may discover order. Outside of such forms lie chaos, madness, and the void. "The House," the narrator observes, "was a world, more real than The Chase, and less exposed; everything beyond its gates was foreign and unimportant and could be ignored." The prospect of returning to the Tulsis becomes particularly attractive when Mr. Biswas thinks of the future: "It was a blankness, a void like those in dreams, into which, past tomorrow and next week and next year, he was falling." After his wife gives birth to their third child, a girl named Myna, Mr. Biswas returns to Hanuman House. His retreat to this ordered world is short-lived, however, for Seth informs him that he needs someone to help oversee a Tulsi sugarcane plantation at Green Vale. It is here that Mr. Biswas comes face to face with the void.

Green Vale is Mr. Biswas's Garden of Gethsemane. Shama and the children spent most of their time at Hanuman House, leaving Mr. Biswas alone in the depressing atmosphere of this godforsaken outpost. Despite its pastoral name, Green Vale is like a wasteland to Mr. Biswas. The trees around the ramshackle barracks where he and the workers live have drooping leaves, "dead green" in color. Green Vale is damp and shadowed and its claustrophobic weight comes to test the strength of Mr. Biswas's mind and spirit. Naipaul describes his hero's state of mind as he enters this new phase of his spiritual maturity: "The future he feared was upon him. He was falling into the void, and that terror, known only in dreams, was with him as he lay awake at nights, hearing the snores and creaks and the occasional cries of babies from the other rooms."

Intensifying Mr. Biswas's anxiety is the growing hostility of the laborers toward him. His isolation gradually makes him paranoid and he begins to imagine that the inanimate objects around him have the potential for violence: the rocker could crush his body, the windows and doors could trap and mangle, and so he lay on his bed covering the vital parts of his body against the nightmarish aggression of his room. His fear of the void and the onset of his mental breakdown, however, are temporarily suspended when he focuses his energies upon obtaining his own house in Green Vale. A house would not only allow him a safe distance from the threatening laborers but the desperately needed peace of mind and independence denied him from childhood. And so, he hires a carpenter to build him a house.

Throughout the novel Mr. Biswas's reach continues to exceed his grasp, and his dream house remains elusive. Having little money, Mr. Biswas winds up with an unsubstantial, half-finished building, with an asphalt roof that melts in the heat and drips into long, black snakelike forms. Like the landscape of Green Vale itself, the description of the rotting house and its nightmarish snakes curling and falling down from the roof suggest the psychological shift within Mr. Biswas. Despite his feelings of failure and humiliation at Hanuman House, at least there he could enjoy the vigor of his ongoing battle with Shama's family. The family house provided a sanctuary from the real world, and now that he is alone, with only his thoughts of failure and his fear of the nothingness both within and without, he is truly an orphan in a violent mental storm. Seized by fear, he turns to his dog and says, "You are an animal and think that because I have a head and hands and look as I did yesterday I am a man. I am deceiving you. I am not whole." Undercutting any sentimentality, Naipaul points out that Mr. Biswas never enjoyed but only imagined a period of golden childhood innocence: "And mixed with his fear was this grief for a happy life never enjoyed and now lost."

Mr. Biswas undergoes his psychological crisis shortly after a visit from Shama. As she is about to leave, Anand is faced with the decision to return to Hanuman House with his mother or stay at Green Vale with his father. He chooses to remain because, as he later explains to Mr. Biswas, "they was going to leave you alone." Although Mr. Biswas was not especially close to the boy in the past, the next few days instill a new and profound intimacy between them. At last he has a child that he can shape and fashion, a young mind out of the reach of Shama and her meddling relatives. He begins to teach the boy about God, science, and painting, and at night they draw imaginary scenes of snow-covered mountains. These paintings reflect Naipaul's own youthful fantasies about snow-covered lands, scenes that he later develops in *The Mimic Men*. They comprise the unfulfilled dreams of his romantic heroes, each of whom is seriously scarred by the jagged edges of the real world that Naipaul delights in honing to surgical sharpness.

In an attempt to gain a new frame of mind, Mr. Biswas and his son move to the finished room in his new house. The asphalt snakes, however, begin to dominate his dreams and his nightmare world begins in earnest to test his mettle. As the snakes continue to grow and infest his imagination, he has Anand chant a Hindu incantation to keep him safe. It is interesting to note that as a boy Mr. Biswas spurned the Hindu ritualistic rites. Now, in his most severe moment of crisis, this relic of the past is all that he can call upon to help control and order the chaos that threatens to overwhelm him. The most oppressive of all his fears, however, is that Anand would leave him and he would be left alone, his paranoid mind and spirit vulnerable to the slightest bruise.

Mr. Biswas's psychological breakdown has its correlative in the violent storm that suddenly comes up. Lightning, thunder, shadows of the asphalt snakes cast upon the wall by the oil lamp, and a huge swarm of winged ants all converge upon the small, fragile house. To make matters worse, Mr. Biswas fears the men in the barracks are about to do him harm, and so he and his boy begin to chant their protective prayer more vigorously. Finally a powerful wind bursts the window open and extinguishes the lamp "and when the lightning went out the room was part of the black void." Naipaul's recurrent reference to the void reaches a climax, marking the point at which both the house and Mr. Biswas's mind merge into total darkness.

When Mr. Biswas comes to his senses he discovers that he has been carried back to Hanuman House. The place that for years he had hated and fought against suddenly becomes his safe harbor, a regulated world that provides the security that he so desperately sacrificed out of his pride in Green Vale. Mr. Biswas "welcomed the warmth and reassurance of the room. Every wall was solid." His surrender to the anguish of the past has finally brought a sort of peace within him. Furthermore, the nightmare experience in Green Vale now affords him hope for the future. The days there "had given him an experience of unhappiness against which everything had now to be measured."

In a limited sense Mr. Biswas has been reborn. Having survived his dark night of the soul, he faces the future with new confidence: "He was going out into the world, to test it for its power to frighten. The past was counterfeit, a series of cheating accidents. Real life, and its especial sweetness, awaited; he was still beginning." As a realist, however, Naipaul makes it clear as the novel proceeds that Mr. Biswas's new beginning, while hopeful and admirable, is not without serious restraints that will hamper and test his hero's indefatigable spirit at every step.

Mr. Biswas starts his new life by moving to Port of Spain and working as an apprentice journalist for the Trinidad *Sentinel.* Strapped for money, he once again finds himself living in the house of another. Mrs. Tulsi, who has moved to Port of Spain to be with her son, allows Mr. Biswas and his family to live in her elegant house. And so, once again, Mr. Biswas finds himself moving within the powerful sphere of influence of his mother-in-law, the paradoxical figure who both nurtures and threatens to overwhelm his individuality. At this point, however, Mr. Biswas is delighted to live in such luxury.

Besides writing sensationalized snippets for the *Sentinel,* Mr. Biswas occasionally attempts composing fiction but does not get past the opening fragment of a story he entitles "Escape": "At the age of thirty-three, when he was already the father of four children. . . ." This unfinished story provides a neat parallel with his own failed attempts to escape from the circumstances that oppress him: the suffocating influence of the Tulsis, his lack of money, the responsibility for a growing family, the failure at the height of his manhood to have carved out a significant place in the world. Mr. Biswas comes to use his opening sentence fragment to test his typewriter whenever he cleans it or changes its ribbon. The sentence remains incomplete even, finally, as does his life.

After Owad, Mrs. Tulsi's son, leaves for England to study medicine, Mrs. Tulsi moves back to Hanuman House. But the influence of the Tulsis is never again the same or as powerful. Mr. Biswas, meanwhile, continues to try to carve out a niche for himself with the newspaper writing accounts of the local court, funerals, and cricket matches. Hope for a brighter future rekindles when the Tulsi family moves to an Edenic spot named Shorthills. Although by living there rent-free Mr. Biswas is able to save his earnings at the paper, he has to witness the family's plunder: trees are cut, machinery dismantled, and everyone is out to serve himself. Mr. Biswas also joins in the plunder by stealing fruit from the trees and selling it in town. All of the chaos stems from the failure of Mrs. Tulsi to continue to rule and control the childlike selfishness of her extended family. Mr. Biswas finally gets a house built for his family away from the main house but his luck, as usual, is blighted and the house burns to the ground. The events at Shorthills, however, confirm the failure of the Tulsis' outmoded Hinduism and communal life style. As Kenneth Ramchand observes, "The object of Naipaul's satire is changing from a static communalism to the new colonial individualism."[4] In times of crisis, even Mr. Biswas acknowledges the comfort and protection afforded by the formal social structure of Hanuman House.

Back in Mrs. Tulsi's house in Port of Spain, Mr. Biswas takes up the pieces of his life again and the *Sentinel* assigns him the task of reading the applications of the destitute, the most deserving of which he writes up in the newspaper. This job, ironically, merely reinforces his personal fears of getting fired, becoming ill, or falling prey to some unexpected disaster. The awful void that lies just beneath the surface of his maddening routines now threatens him daily in the stories he compiles for a living. Naipaul's description of Mr. Biswas's visit to the home of Bhandat, the ostracized brother of the wealthy Ajodha, captures the dark realism that shadows even the happiest moments in this novel. Bhandat, living in poverty, begs Mr. Biswas to write up his case. The sour and stale smell of Bhandat's place overwhelms Mr. Biswas. A deaf and dumb woman living with Bhandat serves him some tea: "The tea had spilled on the bed, on Bhandat. And Mr. Biswas, thinking of deafness, dumbness, insanity, the horror of the sexual act in that grimy room, felt the yellow cake turn to a sweet slippery paste in his mouth. On the bed Bhandat was in a paroxysm of rage, cursing in Hindi" (p. 452).

The last section of the novel begins to focus more on Anand, whose devotion to his studies wins him a scholarship to college. Mr. Biswas, however, continues to suffer humiliations, as when his mother dies and the medical examiner's rude behavior drives Mr. Biswas to write him an indignant eight-page letter. Mr. Biswas also begins to lose hope of ever owning a house of his own: "He sank into despair as into the void which, in his imagining, had always stood for the life he had yet to live." His hopes are revived when he is appointed Community Welfare Officer, a position that gives him a sense of belonging to a new era of postwar development. Armed with a government job, a car, and an actual vacation, Mr. Biswas begins to win back his self respect. Once again, however, his joy is short lived. Owad returns triumphant from England and the Tulsi family comes to life with renewed vigor and influence.

Seth has by now lost his place in the Tulsi hierarchy and Owad, fresh from England, his head full of romantic notions of Marxist solutions to all social ills, takes his position as the new head of household. The entire family falls under his spell, with the exception of Mr. Biswas, who mocks him at every opportunity. Mr. Biswas is intrigued, however, with Owad's statement that in Russia a journalist would be given food, money, and a house. Anand also falls under Owad's influence and begins to parrot his ideas about politics and art until one day Owad mocks and abuses him. At this point, Anand beseeches his father to move away from the Tulsis. When later Mr. Biswas has a heated argument with Mrs. Tulsi, he finally decides the time has come to make a move.

The design of the entire novel now moves to its irrevocable conclusion: Mr. Biswas finally buys his own house. Depressed and having drunk too much, Mr. Biswas meets a man who offers to sell him one of his houses on Sikkim Street. The liquor, the rain, and the night all conspire to make the house look much better than it actually is, but Mr. Biswas is hooked. The pressures of three decades of false starts and failures bear down and distort his judgment and he sets out to make the purchase by borrowing money from his aunt, Tara. For the first time in his life he would be free of the Tulsis.

The house of his lifelong dream turns out to be a miserable structure made of the cheapest materials assembled by the incompetent owner who, it is revealed later, makes a living by selling these low quality houses. But the house is Mr. Biswas's, for better or for worse, and he and the family proceed to make the best of it. Mr. Biswas manages to keep the man who sold him the house from building another structure on the neighboring lot, and in the empty space there Mr. Biswas plants a laburnum tree: "It grew rapidly. It gave the house a romantic aspect, softened the tall graceless lines, and provided some shelter from the afternoon sun. Its flowers were sweet, and in the still hot evenings their smell filled the house" (p. 584).

Through the image of the tree, with its fragrance and romantic addition to the ungainly house, Naipaul suggests Mr. Biswas's final victory, like that of a climber who plants a flag atop a difficult mountain peak. In both the opening chapter and in the epilogue, however, Naipaul makes it very clear that Mr. Biswas is no sentimental or romantic hero. By Western standards the attainment of one's own house is hardly a heroic feat. Given the limits within which Mr. Biswas must work out his destiny, on the other hand, the house acquires a powerful symbolic significance. As Kenneth Ramchand points out, "When Mr. Biswas acquires his house he does not so much create order as confirm its possibility. However wry the accompanying gestures, this is Naipaul's precarious achievement too."[5] Nevertheless, even this significance is tempered by Naipaul's final observations about his hero. The debt on the house remains like an oppressive weight upon Mr. Biswas's mind. His work becomes painful and routine and the articles he writes for the newspaper lose their zest. "Living had always been a preparation, a waiting," Naipaul writes. "And so the years had passed; and now there was nothing to wait for." Having attained his dream, so to speak, Mr. Biswas has lost it. As Browning put it, "A man's reach should exceed his grasp / Or what's a heaven for?" Once a romantic has attained his elusive vision he has nothing left for which to live, except his children.

Savi receives a scholarship and goes abroad. Anand also gets a scholarship and goes to England. Alone now more than ever, Mr. Biswas suffers heart problems and is fired by the *Sentinel.* When he finally dies, the Tulsis crowd the small house: "the staircase shivered continually; the top floor resounded with the steady shuffle. And the house did not fall." Mr. Biswas is cremated and Shama and the children go back to the empty house. With these rather matter-of-fact details Naipaul concludes his story of an ordinary and yet paradoxically remarkable man.

In *A House for Mr. Biswas* Naipaul combines the elements of sympathy and detachment as he explores the humanity of his father and the legacy of rebellion and alienation that he inherited from him. Gordon Rohelhr's observation illuminates the autobiographical subtext of the novel:

> Ostensibly preoccupied with the present, Naipaul observes acculturation as a timeless feature of the West Indian experience which he never really accepts. Like the boy in *Miguel Street,* he rejects the rubbish heap. Like Mr. Biswas, he rejects Hanuman House. Rejecting Hanuman House and Miguel Street as two sides of the greater nightmare of being an Indian in Trinidad, he seeks the freedom of the independent personality, and makes the difficult choice of exile and dispossession. There are few pleasures in his exile. Yet out of it grow irony and a necessary detachment from the nightmare.[6]

Despite this irony and detachment, however, Naipaul manages to suffuse this novel with a glow of human sympathy that more fully surrounds and animates his central character here than in his earlier novels. William Walsh suggests that Naipaul withholds a large part of his own character in the early fiction: "In his first books Naipaul looks at the characters and their world from a distance. . . . But the writing gives the impression that the characters share only a limited part of the author's nature. . . . There is a minor, subservient quality in them, the product of Naipaul's self-contained detachment." In *A House for Mr. Biswas,* on the other hand, Walsh sees the relationship of author and subject as one that exists on a level, as between equals: "Mr. Biswas is felt and suffered with, not just seen and suffered. This mild and charitable acceptance, this capacity to unfold without smudging or distaste, shows itself at every point in the novel, and as clearly as anywhere in the muted, curbed conclusion."[7]

One of the most compelling reasons that Naipaul treats his hero with such understanding and sympathy is that he is based upon that of his own father. Like Mr. Biswas, the senior Naipaul was beset with enormous difficulties in setting the course of his life and that of his family. The parallels between the two figures are extensive. Like Mr. Biswas, who constantly fought against the influence of the Tulsis, the senior Naipaul "was full of rages against my mother's family, a large Brahmin family of landowners and pundits." Naipaul writes that his father, again like Mr. Biswas, was a rebel: "The family, with all its pundits, were defenders of the orthodox Hindu faith. My father wasn't." Mr. Biswas was a journalist for the *Sentinel* and Naipaul's father worked for the Trinidad *Guardian*. Both figures suffered terrible humiliations and both showed signs of serious mental illness—Mr. Biswas at Green Vale, and Naipaul's father during the latter part of his life. Both men read the works of Marcus Aurelius and Epictetus for consolation.

Even as Mr. Biswas experienced his ups and downs on the *Sentinel*, finally getting sacked, Naipaul's father, during his last years with the paper, faced similar tribulations. After Naipaul, Sr., became mentally unbalanced, the new editor of the *Guardian* took him off the staff and reduced him to the position of a stringer. Admiration for his craft as a journalist, however, stayed with him, and he passed this sense of a vocation on to his son. Most important, however, is the legacy of fear that he infused in his son along with the means of combating it. Naipaul writes,

> He never talked about the nature of his illness. And what is astonishing to me is that, with the vocation, he so accurately transmitted to me—without saying anything about it—his hysteria from the time when I didn't know him: his fear of extinction. That was his subsidiary gift to me. That fear became mine as well. It was linked with the idea of the vocation: the fear could be combatted only by the exercise of the vocation.[8]

The character of Anand is associated with Naipaul himself. Both escape the entrapment of Trinidad by winning a scholarship to

England. One of the weaknesses of this novel is that Naipaul fails to develop the relationship between Mr. Biswas and Anand, not to mention the relationship between Mr. Biswas and his other children. One of the possible reasons for this failure is that it was only in 1972, when Naipaul was forty years old, that he obtained "a connected idea" of his father's ancestry and early life. The powerful intimacy that develops between Mr. Biswas and his son at Green Vale, where his fear of extinction and of the void overwhelms him, is never developed. Toward the end of his life Mr. Biswas simply laments his failure to become involved in his children's lives: "I have missed their childhoods."

Given Naipaul's significant investment of his own feelings and attitudes in *A House for Mr. Biswas,* there is still the question of how he shaped those emotions and perceptions into an appropriate form. It is a literary truism that all authors must draw upon tradition for their forms, no matter how radical their achievement. Lacking a literary tradition in Trinidad, Naipaul turned to Europe, and England in particular, for his fictional guides. Robert Hamner argues that although Mr. Biswas may be an archetypal Everyman, he has been modernized and shaped after Camus's absurd man: "In each direction he turns he finds obstacles to his happiness, and he can discover no reason for his predicament. Thus he conforms to Camus's fundamental definition of the 'absurd' which is neither a quality of the world, nor simply an idea born in man, but the result of their being situated together."[9] Hamner goes on to say that this type of literary figure is not uncommon, having been made familiar by such writers as J. D. Salinger, Saul Bellow, and Bernard Malamud. Mr. Biswas not only partakes of this class, Hamner says, but "he also owes a great deal to the nineteenth-century school of social realists, whose leading characters, like Dickens's and Hardy's, exemplify the contemporary society out of which they grow as they attempt to redeem it. Biswas, then, simultaneously embodies the alienated modern man and the sensitive though ineffectual reformer."[10]

Despite the literary tradition that informs this novel, Naipaul was facing an aesthetic problem grounded in his unique cultural background. Kerry McSweeney summarizes this difficulty as follows: "Just as Mr. Biswas's problem is that his society provides no channels for ambition or opportunities for self-definition, the same society provides Naipaul with none of the themes and conflicts that are the meat and drink of the traditional kind of novel he is writing."[11] Thus, as McSweeney points out, because of the rudimentary nature of his society, Mr. Biswas's life appears shapeless and aimless. The novel thereby acquires an episodic quality, making Mr. Biswas something of a picaresque hero, in the manner of Dickens's Mr. Pickwick.

It is interesting to note in this connection that Naipaul, who holds that the involvement of the black Trinidadian with the white world limits his writing and that the black American destroys his writing by focusing upon his blackness, may himself be unwittingly in league with black writers in carving out a major new theme and form rooted in the Third World consciousness. As Gordon Rohlehr observes,

> Naipaul does not realize that in treating the theme of East Indian acculturation, and the reconstruction of the Indian personality in the New World, he is at one with Negro writers who are also trying to reconstruct personality, and is writing a most vital portion of the sensitive history of the West Indies. Naipaul's Mr. Biswas rebels because his society denies him personality and forces him to live with an inferiority complex and a sense of nonentity. Negro writers, in the Caribbean or America, protest because their society annihilated identity. Both in the case of Mr. Biswas and the Negro of the New World, underprivilege is struggling to build its symbolic house against overwhelming odds.[12]

It is not only through the acquisition of a symbolic house, however, that Mr. Biswas attempts to define his world. Like Mr. Stone and Ralph Singh, the heroes of two subsequent novels—not to mention Naipaul himself—Mr. Biswas struggles to assert his identity and shape the chaos of his life through his creative powers. It is no accident that Naipaul makes Mr. Biswas a sign painter and journalist, a person who possesses the rudimentary magic powers of art and language to transform his decaying world into a habitable and accommodating place. It is through his expressive writing that he is able to free himself from the psychological imprisonment of the Tulsis. The unfinished story he spends most of his time on is significantly entitled "Escape." Both his writing and his paintings are ways of escape—from the Tulsis, from Trinidad, and from the inexorable void. From the simple signs he painted for the store at

Hanuman House to the exotic pastoral landscapes he created with Anand at Green Vale, Mr. Biswas possessed the saving power to escape from his actual depressing surroundings. That he never completed his story "Escape" testifies to Naipaul's refusal to sentimentalize his hero's achievement. Mr. Biswas remains the frustrated artist whose dreams are elusive but whose spirit and humanity are never diminished in his quest for order and placidity.

4

Shipwrecked

Naipaul's first travel book, *The Middle Passage,* begun in 1960 and published in 1962, sheds considerable light upon the novels he writes subsequent to *A House for Mr. Biswas.* After this expansive tragicomic novel, Naipaul's vision suddenly narrows and becomes progressively more analytical, detached, cynical, unsympathetic, and often brutal. At the same time his sensibility becomes more intensely focused upon such obsessive themes as death, sexuality, homelessness, failure, and identity. The following passage from James Anthony Froude's *The English in the West Indies* (1887), which Naipaul quotes as his epigraph for *The Middle Passage,* articulates the profound grievance that killed whatever latent joy Naipaul may have recovered from his childhood and that now haunts and shapes the thoughts, structures, and feelings of all his writing:

> They were valued only for the wealth which they yielded, and society there has never assumed any particularly noble aspect. There has been splendour and luxurious living, and there have been crimes and horrors, and revolts and massacres. There has been romance, but it has been the romance of pirates and outlaws. The natural graces of life do not show themselves under such conditions. There has been no saint in the West Indies since Las Casas, no hero unless philonegro enthusiasm can make one out of Toussaint. There are no people there in the true sense of the word, with a character and purpose of their own.[1]

The title of *The Middle Passage* refers to the middle leg of the slave-carrying voyage between Africa and the Caribbean. In this book Naipaul analyzes the way in which the characters of ex-colonies are shaped by their past history. The five societies that

Naipaul explores are Trinidad, British Guiana, Surinam, Martinique, and Jamaica. In giving his impressions of these places, Naipaul goes beyond a documentary account to reveal his strong personal involvement with the colonial wreckage left behind by England, France, and Holland.

Naipaul believes that the West Indian, living in a borrowed culture, requires writers to give him a cultural identity. The imposed British and American social conventions, however, shackle the West Indian writer and deprive his work of international appeal. "The reader is excluded," Naipaul argues; "he is invited to witness; he cannot participate." It is precisely this line of thinking that explains why Naipaul abandoned the form of his early comic novels to attempt a more critical and analytical novel such as *A House for Mr. Biswas* and to move away from his Caribbean setting in *Mr. Stone and the Knights Companion.*

By the early 1960s Naipaul became convinced that his colonial world was a sick one and that a writer is obligated to go beyond merely re-creating that world, he must diagnose its disease. "No writer," he says, "can be blamed for reflecting his society. If the West Indian writer is to be blamed, it is because, by accepting and promoting the unimpressive race-and-colour values of his group, he has not only failed to diagnose the sickness of his society but has aggravated it" (*MP,* p. 70). Naipaul attempts to put this idea into practice with *The Mimic Men,* a probing analysis of the mind of a failed Caribbean politician.

If Naipaul seems obsessed in his later novels with the theme of failure, this theme evolves directly out of his observations in *The Middle Passage.* The societies he describes in this work are all fundamentally flawed by their colonial pasts. They are degraded and humiliated worlds lacking a cultural or political integrity. In his fiction Naipaul's favorite metaphor for the abandoned ex-colonial is that of the shipwreck victim. Froude's painful assessment that in the West Indies there are no people with a character and purpose of their own describes the unhealing wound in Naipaul's vision, a wound that eventually contracts his broad outlook on humanity in *A House for Mr. Biswas* to a laserlike focus upon the elements of dislocation, brutality, and despair in his subsequent works.

The colorful and, at times, Edenic Trinidad of *Miguel Street, The Mystic Masseur,* and *The Suffrage of Elvira* is transformed in *The Middle Passage* into a wasteland of shame and degradation. Naipaul characterizes his homeland as "unimportant, uncreative, cynical," a place where "dignity was allowed to no one," where every person of distinction "was held to be crooked and contemptible." A society that denies itself heroes, Trinidad lacks a communal identity. Only in the fact that it belongs to the British Empire does it have any identity. Port of Spain, its capital, is remembered for being the "noisiest city in the world," full of blaring radios. American movies dominate the culture and Trinidadians remake themselves into the images of "the Hollywood B-man." The only standards of the Trinidadian are wit and style.

Naipaul's portrait of Jamaica is equally depressing. In describing the slums of Kingston, Jamaica, he reveals not only his bitterness at this colonial wreckage but his eye for the brutal dehumanizing detail that later characterizes his fiction. After noting the filth and rubbish that are disgorged everywhere, the pigs and goats wandering among the packing-case houses, he concludes: "Against such a view lay a dead mule, its teeth bared, its belly swollen and taut. It had been there for two days; a broomstick had been playfully stuck in its anus" (*MP,* p. 216).

Like the Trinidadians, the Jamaicans have no sense of identity. The Rastafarians dream of returning to Africa or Ethiopia. Naipaul expresses his deep disappointment with the illiterate black men who foolishly shout for racial redemption. "They've destroyed their little world," he says. "I never thought that after 300 years of the new world an African people could return to the bush. That is very sad."[2]

Wherever he looks, he is saddened, embittered. Arriving in Martinique he feels as if he has crossed not the Caribbean but the English Channel: "They are black, but they are Frenchmen." He finds that the hard social prejudices of the metropolitan bourgeoisie "have coalesced with the racial distinctions derived from slavery to produce the most organized society in the West Indies." But it is an organization that benefits the French, not the natives. "Assimilation has not made Martinique an integral part of prosperous France, but has reduced the island to a helpless colony where now more than ever the commission agent is king" (p. 199).

The poverty, exploitation, racial strife, degradation, and lack of cultural identity that Naipaul explores in these societies are personal as well as historic wounds. Out of the pain of this recognition he begins to elaborate the theme developed in *A House for Mr. Biswas*, man in search of a home, and widens it to man in search of his country or his identity. Unlike Alex Haley, who romanticized his historical background in *Roots*, Naipaul emphasizes the brutal reality of his dislocation. His return to Trinidad and his subsequent analysis of the place of his birth prove to be stifling psychological adventures. The problems are clearly diagnosed but he has no solutions to offer.

In his next travel book, *An Area of Darkness*, Naipaul follows the next logical route to his past and visits India, the home of his grandfather. Although the book was not published until 1964, it is important to realize that Naipaul visited India to begin work on it in 1961, only a year after his unhappy return to Trinidad. *The Middle Passage* and *An Area of Darkness*, then, suggest Naipaul's compelling need to discover how he fits into the world around him. The two books represent Naipaul's disappointed pilgrimage toward self-discovery. Everywhere he looks he continues to see self-violation, filth, degradation, humiliation. He is obsessed with the Indians who defecate openly along the roads, and his eye for such detail quickly recalls the image of the dead mule with the broomstick "playfully inserted in its anus" that he noted in Kingston. Like the Trinidadians lacking writers to help them know who they are, the Indians have willingly corrupted themselves with Western ideas: "Indian attempts at the novel further reveal the Indian confusion. The novel is of the West. . . . It is part of the mimicry of the West, the Indian self-violation."

Despite his travels throughout India during the course of a year, Naipaul's final assessment of his voyage is a cynical one, a disillusionment: "In a year I had not learned acceptance. I had learned my separateness from India, and was content to be a colonial, without a past, without ancestors." The India of his childhood imaginings is left to remain just that—a fantasy, a land of myth, "an area of darkness." In the India of the present, however, he discovers a congenial "philosophy of despair, leading to passivity, detachment, acceptance" and recognizes it as one that helps to define his own developing attitudes that sanction his withdrawal from the social and national loyalties of his past. His ventures into the West Indies and India accentuate his brooding vision of despair, his profound sense of innocence and hope lost in a cruel historical shipwreck that left his Brahmin grandfather stranded on a Caribbean island without character, purpose, or identity.

In both *Mr. Stone and the Knights Companion* and *The Mimic Men* Naipaul attempts to deal with some of the powerful and painful issues he raises in his two travel books. His total repression of Caribbean character and setting in *Mr. Stone and the Knights Companion* has usually been viewed as a tour de force, a sort of literary statement that he is a citizen of the world no longer bound by the stifling limits shared by other Third World writers. While there is certainly some truth to such an assessment, there seems to be another strategy at work in this novel. By eliminating the cultural signs and symbols of his past, Naipaul can focus exclusively and intensely upon the mind and character of the displaced person. The novel is about human connections: Mr. Stone's relationship to his organization, to his friends, to his neighbors, to the cycles of life. In order to gain control over his life and give it meaning, the isolated hero finally resorts to writing. *The Mimic Men,* on the other hand, extends many of the concerns of Mr. Stone and fleshes them out with specific references to the Caribbean and the issues of cultural dislocation and despair.

Mr. Stone and the Knights Companion

In writing *Mr. Stone and the Knights Companion,* Naipaul abandons the broad range of characters and expanse of time that characterized *A House for Mr. Biswas* in favor of an intense, narrowed, and analytical focus upon a single consciousness. Told from the perspective of the omniscient author, the novel makes a break from the Caribbean world of Naipaul's earlier works as it examines the last two years before retirement of the thoroughly British head librarian of a company named Excal. Naipaul explains that he chose to write this novel as a reaction to the luxuriance of *A House for Mr. Biswas.* His plan was to write "a compressionist novel pared to the bone."[3]

Many critics, fascinated with Naipaul's Caribbean background, have welcomed his surprising show of versatility in developing an English character and setting for this novel. It seems to me, however, much more significant that Naipaul in this and his next novel, *The Mimic Men,* becomes obsessed with the subject of death and the supreme importance of order and control in one's life as a means of attaining peace and self knowledge. The setting of these two novels is of secondary importance. Richard Stone, Englishman, and Ralph Singh, Caribbean, share fundamental human concerns: they are afraid of dying, they desperately seek to maintain or create order in their lives, and they yearn for peace and detachment, a solace for their frail, corruptible flesh.

In working with these themes through two books, Naipaul also develops a writer's self-reflexiveness. Mr. Stone achieves his greatest adventure from his writing a proposal for dealing humanely with retirees of Excal, and Ralph Singh salvages his fragmented identity through writing his memoirs. Fundamental to the themes of both novels is T. S. Eliot's expression of the disparity between thought and action: "Between the idea / And the reality / Between the motion / And the act / Falls the shadow" ("The Hollow Men"). These lines may well have served as the epigraphs for both of Naipaul's novels. Commenting upon Stone's proposal of the Knights Companion as a project written out of a "pure" moment, Naipaul paraphrases Eliot: "What he had written was a faint and artificial rendering of that emotion, and the scheme as . . . practiced . . . was but a shadow of that shadow."

The novel opens with a wonderfully comic scene in which the fastidious Mr. Stone, who despises and fears the neighbor's black cat that daily assaults his small garden, lays an intricate trail of cheese from the yard into his house, up the stairs, and into the bathroom where he waits, poker in hand, to murder his old enemy. After sitting there waiting some ten minutes, he suddenly remembers "it was rats that ate cheese. Cats ate other things." As will be seen, Mr. Stone's feline adversary becomes an important symbolic figure later in his life, not unlike the sea snakes that Coleridge's Ancient Mariner at first abhors but subsequently blesses as an extension of himself.

Seemingly a confirmed bachelor, Mr. Stone lives in a rundown house cared for by an old housekeeper named Miss Millington. He has worked for Excal for thirty years and soon faces retirement. Locked comfortably within the strict routines of his life, this timid, proper man, reminiscent of Eliot's Prufrock, appears destined to remain the stereotype of the "little man" of English literature, like Mr. Pooter or Boffin. Thoughts of death and an invitation to a party, however, soon change the course of his life.

At the annual dinner party of his friends Tony and Grace Tomlinson Mr. Stone meets a middle-aged widow named Margaret Springer. He subsequently invites her to tea at his house on two occasions and, in a sentence, Naipaul simply announces that "in the second week of March Mr. Stone and Mrs. Springer were married." Commenting on this abrupt narrative development, V. S. Pritchett writes, "In all his novels and in this one most of all, Naipaul gives us people suspended—as they are in Mr. Stone's fantasies—and without dynamic principle: we do not know why or how Mr. Stone gets married. He marries out of the blue—just as Mr. Biswas was married against his will. In both cases the parties are indifferent to each other. They have had no youth, no rising sap. When they act it is by accident in the midst of anxious lassitude."[4] Naipaul says that in his first draft of the novel he married off Mr. Stone in one sentence. His explanation, one hardly acceptable to Pritchett, is as follows: "A man reaches a certain age, he wants to get married, he gets married; what more is there to say?—but then I thought that was going too far and so gave his courtship half a page."[5]

In his attempt to write a highly economical novel and to focus tightly upon his hero's quiet desperation, Naipaul occasionally fails to establish human relationships. It may well be, of course, that he is so obsessed with working out his own problems that his heroes are not, in fact, concerned with other people except insofar as they serve their needs. This certainly seems to be the case with Ralph Singh in *The Mimic Men,* an unabashed egoist whose character has been prepared for by Mr. Stone.

Naipaul employs several symbols to reflect Mr. Stone's growing anxiety over his impending retirement and death. One is a tree in the school grounds at the back of his house "by which he noted the passing of time." He studies the tree from his window every morning while shaving: "The contemplation of this living object assured him of the solidity of things. He had grown to regard it as part of his own life, a marker of his past, for it moved through time with him." Up to this point the tree merely reminded him of his mounting experience and his deepening past, not of time running out or death.

The notion of his own death first appears as a "faint unease" provoked by his observance of his two distant neighbors whom he has dehumanized with the names "The Male" and "The Monster." The former is a small man with a large family who is always hanging out of windows, painting, sawing, hammering, "making improvements to his nest." The latter is an enormously fat woman who hibernates in winter and waters her garden all spring and summer. In contrast to these grotesque and industrious restorers of life, Mr. Stone takes a perverse delight in the slow decay of his own house. Watching the neighbors, the tree, contemplating his own situation, his coming retirement, his dwindling days, Mr. Stone experiences "a twinge of alarm, for it seemed that all the ordered world was threatened."

Mr. Stone begins to see his own fleshly mortality reflected within his housekeeper: "He persuaded himself, as he had never done before, that the woman before him, slowed down by age and by flesh which was bulky but not robust, was soon to die." His routines upset by the Christmas season, Mr. Stone feels that "for a whole week life was dislocated." The growing sense of his own mortality is given new focus in a phrase he reads in a London Transport poster: "*Those who doubt the coming of Spring.*" Even his annual visit to his sister and her ugly daughter fails to distract him from his newfound awareness of death.

While it is true that Naipaul does not prepare the reader for Mr. Stone's marriage, he does develop his hero's growing anxiety over death to the point where his sudden marriage may be read as a desperate move to insulate himself from the devastating notion of retirement as a prelude to death and nothingness. In any event, he settles rather comfortably into his marriage, his fear that marriage might be "a lifelong and exhausting violation of his personality" proving false. Unlike most of Naipaul's male–female relationships, this one is rather pleasant and accommodating. There are no powerful sexual feelings to create the usual contempt, violence, and guilt of Naipaul's male heroes.

During the course of his observation of the tree, the Male, and the Monster reproaching him with the passage of time, Mr. Stone begins to sense something new to him: "all that was not flesh was irrelevant to man, and all that was important was man's own flesh, his weakness and corruptibility." This rather dismal view of human nature, a godless world without hope or spirit, is reiterated in several of Naipaul's novels. The gray comic tone of the novel, combined with the hero's genteel and civilized behavior, softens the dark view. In *The Mimic Men*, however, Naipaul carries the theme of flesh, weakness, and corruptibility to greater heights of despair and emptiness within the dislocated mind of Ralph Singh, Mr. Stone's literary descendant.

Typical of Naipaul's heroes, Mr. Stone is an egoist, a person who absorbs the world around him and shapes that world into his own image. Before long both Margaret and Miss Millington "he now saw . . . as extensions of himself." His sense of order begins to get restored as "his habits were converted into rituals" and "grew sacred to him." Naipaul's obsession with the idea of order, control, solidity, apparent in nearly all of his fiction, is reflected in Mr. Stone's defenses against mortality. But these defenses, like Mr. Biswas's house or Singh's memoirs, are inadequate in a world of mere flesh and corruption, and Mr. Stone experiences a horrific revelation during his holiday visit to Cornwall, the land of magic. Mr. Stone and Margaret during one of their outings see a man walk into a burning field and disappear into the smoke. As the smoke dissipates, it seems as if there has been no fire at all, and the man is gone. The event imprints itself upon Mr. Stone's deepest consciousness: "That hallucinatory moment, when earth and life and senses had been suspended, remained with him. It was like an experience of nothingness, an experience of death."

Mr. Stone's greatest defense against the idea of retirement and his personal mortality is his conception of the Knights Companion, a proposal he submits to his employer for organizing an outreach program for retirees of Excal. Naipaul's satiric tone here is too heavy in its Arthurian allusions. The Knights Companion comes across as a Waugh-like parody of big business' attempt to be humane. Besides the Knights who visit the retired employees, there is the annual dinner at which an outstanding Knight is presented the Excalibur sword. Even Mr. Stone's name has an Arthurian ring, suggesting the depository of the magical sword.

The creation of the Knights Companion, not its practical function and administration, is what thrills Mr. Stone and gives him a sense of hope and purpose. Ironically, the idea also proves to be his great disillusionment:

> Nothing that was pure ought to be exposed. And now he saw that in the project of the Knights Companion which had contributed so much to his restlessness, the only pure moments were those he had spent in the study, writing out of a feeling whose depth he realized only as he wrote. What he had written was a faint and artificial rendering of that emotion, and the scheme as the Unit had practised it was but a shadow of that shadow.[6]

Naipaul's romantic theme is that the ineffable dream world of man will inevitably be corrupted as it is translated into words, the public domain, but even more dramatically corrupted as it is converted into action. Nevertheless, Naipaul describes the act of writing as a moment of joy and illumination. Mr. Stone understands the depth of his feeling only as he writes. Furthermore, Naipaul records that "by his work . . . of creating out of an idea—words written on paper in his study—an organization of real people, Mr. Stone never ceased to be thrilled." Faced with the stark reality of death and the absurdity and disorder of existence, can a writer achieve a measure of understanding, significance, calm, or happiness through his writing? Naipaul implies that question both here and in *The Mimic Men* and offers no clear answer.

Mr. Stone's life reaches a new crisis when he learns that his friend Tony Tomlinson has died. Once again events assert the absurdity and fragility of life. Mr. Stone begins to alter his perception of his neighbor's cat, the one he tried to lure into his bathroom with cheese at the opening of the novel. He is now consumed by the cat's idle elegance and by its loneliness. He feels that the cat comes to watch for him every morning even as he comes to watch for it. In short he sees the cat, as earlier he saw Margaret and Miss Millington, as an extension of himself. When he discovers that his new neighbors plan to have the cat destroyed, Mr. Stone sadly says to it, "You will soon be dead. Like me." When it is later destroyed, he becomes filled with self-disgust and fear.

The final impact of Mr. Stone's traumatic experiences during the past two years leads him to assume a cynical philosophy. "All action, all creation," he feels, "was a betrayal of feeling and truth." And in the process of this betrayal Mr. Stone's "world had come tumbling about him." Naipaul summarizes his hero's final dark insight into reality:

> All that mattered was man's own frailty and corruptibility. The order of the universe, to which he had sought to ally himself, was not his order . . . now he saw, too, that it was not by creation that man demonstrated his power and defied this hostile order, but by destruction. By damming the river, by destroying the mountain, by so scarring the face of the earth that Nature's attempt to reassert herself became a mockery. (p. 125)

Commenting upon this passage, V. S. Pritchett writes: "Anyone with will and vigour left in him would say the very opposite: construction." He goes on to say that this view weakens his work, that "Naipaul's observation inclines him to weariness and is at odds with his imagination. His mistrust of the continuous constructing will may be something he gets from his Hindu upbringing in the Caribbean and from the fact that he is a doubly displaced person: displacement is aging. The colonial sadness is not ours."[7]

There seems to be more than sadness in this passage. The very language and its powerful rhetorical force ("demonstrated . . . defied . . . destruction . . . damming . . . destroying") reveal a violent hostility aimed at nature's status quo. The theme of violence that runs through Naipaul's books, culminating in the brutal murder and sodomy in *Guerrillas,* reveals the rage and frustration of such recurrent "little men" as Mr. Biswas, Mr. Stone, and Jimmy Ahmed. Surely these emotions have been tested by Naipaul himself in his obsession with his inferior background, with his sense of alienation, and with his years of failure to find a large, appreciative, and understanding audience for his stories.

Mr. Stone's dark thoughts are somewhat lightened in the last page of the novel. As he is about to enter his house he sees the green eyes of a cat in his hall: "Fear blended into guilt, guilt into love." He calls out, "Pussy," but the young black cat runs out the door before he can make another move. He thus greets his new feline adversary with compassion and understanding. Mr. Stone "was no destroyer," one is told. "Once before the world had collapsed about him. But he had survived. And he had no doubt that in time calm would come to him again."

The novel seems to end, then, in a state of confusion. Within the space of a few paragraphs Naipaul moves his hero from philosophical considerations of destruction and open warfare with the order of the universe to the acceptance of his fate and of the comfortable routines that order and give meaning to his fragile, corruptible flesh.

A Flag on the Island

The title novelette in a collection of short stories, *A Flag on the Island* was written in 1965 but published in 1967. Most of Naipaul's critics do not have very much to say about this work, except to note its unusual style. As with *Mr. Stone and the Knights Companion,* Naipaul chooses a foreign narrator, in this instance, an American named Frank. He also employs a form of stream of consciousness in order to convey Frank's swirling thoughts as he revisits a Caribbean island where he was stationed years ago during World War II.

A passenger aboard a tourist liner, Frank and his fellow travelers are forced by hurricane Irene to dock at an unnamed West Indian island until the storm passes. Although Frank has given much thought to his former life on the island, he has deliberately steered away from ever returning to it, fearing that his memories of old friends and associates would be violated by a revisitation. One need only to recall Naipaul's own fear of returning to Trinidad in 1960 to find the source of his fictional hero here. Writing in *The Middle Passage* he says, "I never examined this fear of Trinidad. I had never wished to. In my novels I had only expressed this fear; and it is only now, at the moment of writing, that I am able to attempt to examine it." What he says here is not entirely true, for *A Flag on the Island* certainly is an attempt to understand this fear. The fact that Naipaul has chosen an American for his narrator attests to his attempt to arrive at an outsider's point of view, an attempt, however impossible, to stand outside of himself and superimpose the past upon the present of a failing culture.

Frank begins his story with an expression of fear that the inviolate sense of the past may be contaminated by the sordidness of the present, a fear that the tale bears out: "It was an island around which I had been circling for some years. My duties often took me that way and I could have called there any time. But in my imagination the island had ceased to be accessible; and I wanted it to remain so."[8] Nevertheless, the unscheduled arrival of the tropical storm forces Frank to come to grips with a past purified by memory and imagination. Mr. Blackwhite, a local writer, used to say, "This place doesn't exist," and Frank, recognizing the wisdom of that remark, observes that the island is actually a place each person constructs out of his own imagination. The union jack no longer flies here, having been replaced by the island's own flag, but Frank discerns no significant national character here: "The island was a floating suspended place to which you brought your own flag if you wanted to."

All that Frank sees and hears declares the corruption of the past. His old stomping ground, Henry's place, has vanished, with the slick nightclub called the Coconut Grove now serving the locals and tourists; Priest, the tall bearded itinerant prophet, has become a popular television personality named Gary Priestland; and Selma, Frank's gentle and sensitive mistress, now lives with Priestland in the suburbs. Frank tours the island stunned by the caricatures of the past, and then, in the second section of his tale, he retreats to his comfortable and inviolable memories of the past.

After Frank returns to the section of town in which his old house used to stand, he begins to reflect on the annihilated past. His focus is upon Henry's place, a gathering spot for local characters, reminiscent of those depicted in *Miguel Street,* a group of simple people with no past who rely upon style and eccentricity to make their mark. "I don't belong here," Henry says to Frank. "I am like you." It is on the street outside of Henry's place that Frank first meets Priest: "He was a man in love with his own fluency. His accent was very English." Naipaul has already observed in his early stories that a facility with the language wins the respect of and a certain amount of power over others. Followed by a small troupe of young girls singing hymns, Priest moves through the streets collecting money, a scene that foreshadows his later commercial success on television that brings a wider audience. But even at this point his preaching is related to financial matters, for he sells insurance when he is not frightening people about death.

Frank's meeting with the unattached and cool Selma leads to a discussion of Priest. Selma is impressed with Priest's manner of speaking: "I always like hearing a man use language well." It is a sign that he is an educated man, a rarity among the people at Henry's place. Selma herself has been educated and over the years drifted from one relationship to another. "She feared marriage," Frank concludes, "because marriage, for a girl of the people, was full of perils and quick degradation." She and Frank settle into a relationship with the understanding that each one is free to do what he or she wants.

Through Frank's discussions with the writer, Blackwhite, Naipaul examines a fundamental concern in his own writing, namely, how to transform his mundane island life into fiction when the creative center of gravity for the novel lies in England. Frank tells Blackwhite that he is not black at all, that he is terribly white: "You are English. All those lords and ladies, Blackwhite. All that Jane Austen." Frank urges him to abandon writing second-rate romantic novels and to write about the island, about Selma and Henry and the others. Blackwhite's response echoes Naipaul's own fear about his Trinidadian stories: "But you think they will want to read about these people? These people don't exist, you know. . . . This place, I tell you, is nowhere. It doesn't exist. People are just born here. They all want to go away." If Churchill were born here, Blackwhite continues, he would have wound up importing sewing machines and exporting cocoa.

Living up to the other half of his name, Blackwhite gradually comes around to Frank's way of thinking and announces that what he needs is his own language and that he intends to write in patois: "Not English, not French, but something we have made up. This is our own. You were right. Damn those lords and ladies. Damn Jane Austen. This is ours, this is what we have to work with." And thus the fluctuating Blackwhite puts out a notice on his house that reads "Patois taught here." Beneath the comedy of these scenes again lies Naipaul's dilemma as a novelist. Faced with a poverty-stricken culture made up of local characters shaped by the political and economic winds of Europe and America on the one hand, and the rich and domineering tradition of the English novel on the other, how does the writer proceed? The move from the eccentric characters and patois of *Miguel Street* and *The Suffrage of Elvira* to the universal theme of the quest for identity and a sense of place in *A House for Mr. Biswas* to the English persona and his quiet struggle against his mortality in *Mr. Stone and the Knights Companion* represents Naipaul's own progressive struggle to work his way out of this dilemma.

Frank's pleasant memories of the island's local characters and his involvement with them are quickly displaced in a few pages as he chronicles the departure of the American troops and the arrival of the white tourist boats that begin the final destruction of the island's identity. "No place for us now. Change, change. It was fast and furious," Frank reflects. In the third section of the story Frank confronts the degradations that time has wrought upon the island.

Blackwhite's decision to write about the blacks in their own language has ironically led to his corruption. Various foundations have sought him out to support his studies, having brought him to Cambridge and various lecture halls. Naipaul's satire here is rather heavy-handed, as he depicts three foundation representatives named Bippy, Chippy, and Tippy fawning on Blackwhite, eager to support his every foolish novel. When Blackwhite tells them that he is thinking of writing an experimental novel in which a black man falls in love with a black woman, the obsequious trio exclaim, "You'll have the liberals down your throat." They, and the mindless public, want more novels like *I Hate You*, in which he excoriates the white world. Naipaul here channels his disgust with the formulaic and exploitative native fiction, sponsored by American and European foundations, into blunt satire. Money, success, and fame have degraded and undermined the ambiguous Blackwhite, the author without a center of creative consciousness, without roots, and without any cultural identity.

Henry's place has become the Coconut Grove, run by a board of governors, and Henry himself has been awarded the Order of the British Empire. When Frank asks Henry about Selma, Henry says,

Forget Selma. Sometimes you want the world to end. You can't go back and do things again. They begin just like that, they get good. The only thing is you never know they good until they finish. I wish the hurricane would come and blow away all this. I feel the world need this sort of thing every now and then. A clean break, a fresh start. (*FI*, p. 213).

Like Frank, Henry enjoys "moving backwards" instead of moving with the times. He is the spokesman of Naipaul's own view that one does not fully understand or appreciate a quiet, supportive, friendly landscape—a paradise of sorts—until it has vanished. True paradise, then, resides only in the memories of evanescent worlds. Naipaul develops and explores this observation in great detail in a much later work, *The Enigma of Arrival*. Here, however, the focus turns upon annihilation of the present as the final pages chronicle a *danse macabre*.

Frank visits Selma in her modern suburban home equipped with swimming pool and contemporary furnishings. Frank characterizes it as a "lovely, ghastly, sickening, terrible home." He goes to bed with her but too much drink makes him impotent. In the background of this section of the story is Gary Priestland on the television announcing death and destruction from the hurricane. The city becomes convulsed with dancing: "The world was ending and the cries that greeted this end were cries of joy. We all began to dance." In the *danse macabre* all of the figures from the past and present gather together in anticipation of the apocalyptic climax, but the hurricane does not arrive. The exhausted people readjust themselves to their ordinary fates, and Frank returns to his hotel to await the sailing of his ship back home.

Clearly not one of Naipaul's major works, *A Flag on the Island* nevertheless contains a perceptive analysis of the writer's anguish over his lost world. Naipaul's confrontation with his fear of returning to Trinidad has created an interesting piece of fiction that accommodates even though it does not dismiss that fear. The failure of the hurricane to destroy the corrupted island parallels the inadequacy of the author's infantile wish fulfillment that would obliterate his own degraded Trinidad. The anticlimax of the story leaves the harsh residue of reality to be dealt with in later fiction. The childhood innocence of Frank's first arrival is corrupted by his second arrival. Like the naive child, Frank has made the island sacred by filling it with wonder years ago, and now, having come out of the nightmare of the present, has, like the novelist, secured his unrecognized paradise in memories, in words.

The Mimic Men

The narrator of *The Mimic Men* (1967) is Ralph Singh, a forty-year-old West Indian colonial minister living in exile in a suburban London hotel, where he is writing his memoirs in an attempt to impose order upon the chaotic events of his life. "To be born on an island like Isabella," he writes, "an obscure New World transplantation, secondhand and barbarous, was to be born to disorder." His narrative moves in nonchronological fashion between his life in the West Indies and England, between the past and the present, childhood and adulthood, and fantasy and reality in a ruthlessly matter-of-fact and desperate attempt to piece together the fragments of his life, thereby arriving at a clearer understanding of himself. Although Naipaul denies a close kinship to his narrator, he admits that both he and Singh deal with the same psychological problem: "Writing is always a lonely occupation: you have no models, what do you do? That is why I'm particularly pleased with 'The Mimic Men': it deals with my own problem, the disassociation of a man from the simplicity around him."[9]

The novel opens in London shortly after World War II, when Singh is a student at an unnamed institution. He is living in a boardinghouse owned by a Mr. Shylock and when the owner dies during the winter, Singh sees his first snowfall, a moment rich in symbolic significance. Since childhood he has fashioned in his imagination a role of knightly leadership in lands of horsemen, high plains, mountains, and snow. Snow is something he has only read and heard about during his youth in Isabella, the drab Caribbean island of his birth. His excitement, however, quickly cools as he enters the attic room of Mr. Shylock (a room where Mr. Shylock used to meet his young girlfriend) and observes the city from a height suitable to his detached mood: "I felt all the magic of the city go away and had an intimation of the forlornness of the city and the people who lived in it." He then discovers a photograph of an innocent looking, plumpish girl—Mr. Shylock's lover—and seeks to preserve the picture, to protect it, and in so doing, perhaps, to protect himself.

Singh's first experience of snow is thus interlaced with his first experience of death. "Let it not happen to me," he thinks, "Let my relics be honoured. Let me not be mocked." He concludes this opening moment of his memoirs with a statement that sets forth one of the book's major themes: "I knew that my own journey, scarcely begun, had ended in the shipwreck which all my life I had sought to avoid."

One of the central themes of Singh's complex memoirs is the necessity of creating order out of chaos, of gaining a sense of intelligent control over his disordered experiences. While his youthful fantasies help to sustain him in times of crisis, the actual world of politics and sex merely reinforces in him a profound sense of dislocation. About twenty years old when Mr. Shylock died, Singh feels that the past years—during which time he was married, involved in important real-estate dealings and later political leadership in Isabella—"have occurred in parentheses." "Which is the reality?" he asks. "The mood, or the action in between, resulting from that mood and leading up to it again?"

An important aspect of this novel is the tone that Naipaul creates and sustains for his narrator. Singh appears to be remarkably detached from the subject matter of his own life. The voice of the novel is one of calm analysis, matter-of-factness, almost dreariness. It is as if Singh cups his hands around the dying embers of his past and gently blows on them to keep their glow alive as he meditates on their significance. As he says, "My present urge is, in the inaction imposed on me, to secure the final emptiness." The act of writing his memoirs provides him the final solution to his sense of dislocation, for through writing he is at last able to take control of the fragments of his past and shape them into a spiritual and psychological autobiography. His failures in marriage, sex, politics, and business—his twenty years of parenthetical existence that denied the truth of his fantasies—can at last be controlled and given shape in words, paragraphs, and chapters. The memoirs enable Singh to re-create himself in language, leaving him with "the final emptiness" that an author experiences upon the completion of a major work.

In a 1971 interview Naipaul makes a comment on his writing that sheds light upon the significance of Singh's memoirs and his search for the "final emptiness." "Writing," Naipaul says, "is just a sort of disease, a sickness. It's a form of incompleteness. It's a form of anguish. It's despair."[10] Ralph Singh is a dark reflection of Naipaul himself, writing in various small London apartments about his early joyless days. Although he may have experienced anguish and despair during those times, his writing at least offered him an intelligent, controlling form that invested even his emptiness with artistic significance.

There is, however, another emptiness within this novel, a spiritual despondency and frustration of the sort recorded in the early poetry of T. S. Eliot. The very title of the novel suggests Eliot's poem "The Hollow Men." Without a cultural or spiritual heritage of its own, Trinidad is Naipaul's wasteland, a place of "Shape without form, shade without colour, / Paralyzed force, gesture without motion." The voice that speaks at the end of *The Waste Land* most accurately informs the tone and structure of *The Mimic Men*: "These fragments I have shored against my ruins." The fact that Naipaul does not acknowledge Eliot as a major influence upon his work may, indeed, be indicative of his extraordinary indebtedness to him. As a young man infatuated with British culture and who saw London as a literary mecca, Naipaul could not have escaped the Siren lure of Eliot's startling disclosure of his alienation and his clear dramatization of his disordered world. Furthermore, Eliot's obsession with the richness of a mythical past that made the present seem all that more sordid must have had a great appeal to Naipaul, who constantly depicts the empty life in Trinidad as a parody of the rich British culture.

The following passage is a good illustration of Naipaul's reshaping of Eliot's desperate view of London:

> How right our Aryan ancestors were to create gods. We seek sex, and are left with two private bodies on a stained bed. The larger erotic dream, the god, has eluded us. It is so whenever, moving out of ourselves, we look for extensions of ourselves. It is with cities as it is with sex. We seek the physical city and find only a conglomeration of private cells. In the city as nowhere else we are reminded that we are individuals, units. Yet the idea of the city remains; it is the god of the city that we pursue, in vain.[11]

Singh's attempts to overcome his loneliness and isolation through sex prove disastrous. After several encounters with different women,

Singh abandons his sexual adventures after spending a night with a German Swiss woman, with whom he had left an Isabella dollar-note. The next morning he receives a brief message from her, containing the dollar. He is shocked at the clear-sightedness of her note—no "dear," no "love." He senses that she has perceived the absurdity and wrongness of their relationship. In Naipaul's other novels, sex is rarely portrayed in a positive light, and here it is depicted with a revulsion reminiscent of Jonathan Swift's Gulliver:

> Intimacy: the word holds the horror. I could have stayed forever at a woman's breasts, if they were full and had a hint of weight that required support. But there was the skin, there was the smell of skin. There were bumps and scratches, there were a dozen little things that could positively enrage me. . . . Intimacy: it was violation and self-violation. (p. 25)

The image of a nurturing mother, with full, satisfying breasts, is displaced here by the parodic image of imperfect flesh that cannot fulfill Singh's fantasy. European culture had invaded and violated his small island world and now the seductive bodies of European women serve to reenact that grotesque and painful relationship. It is shortly after this sexual anxiety that Singh finds himself longing for the "the certainties of my life on the island of Isabella, certainties which I had once dismissed as shipwreck." Nevertheless, his restlessness leads him to continued self-violation and self-disgust through a series of encounters with prostitutes. "The crash was coming," he notes.

Commenting on the present, the time of his writing the memoirs, Singh takes pleasure in the physical surroundings of the old hotel in which he lives and writes. "For here is order of a sort," he writes. "But it is not mine. It goes beyond my dream. In a city already simplified to individual cells this order is a further simplification. It is rooted in nothing; it links to nothing." Still, compared with the sexual and psychic disorder of his early days when he was overcome by "the panic of ceasing to feel myself as a whole person," the quiet, regulated life of the hotel provides a pleasant atmosphere, conducive for someone attempting to re-create himself as a whole person, at least in fiction.

The opening of chapter 4 gives a clear sense of the narrator's consistently cool and detached tone: "In the active period of my life, which I have described as a period in parentheses, marriage was an episode; and it was the purest accident that I should have entered politics almost as soon as this marriage came to an end." After one of his bouts of restlessness, Singh returned to London in a rather desperate mood. It was during such a stressful time that he met Sandra, a fellow student, who provided him a sense of peace and fulfillment.

Sandra, like many of the other characters in this novel, fails to come alive. Naipaul gives a diminished sense of the characters surrounding his semiautobiographical narrator. Singh the writer is the center of his small universe now and he grants life to those around and part of him only insofar as they provide links in his self-analysis. Sandra, for example, is introduced to the reader in terms of her breasts. Singh devotes a whole page of description to her body, especially to "the fullness of her breasts." He is obsessed with their "weight just threatening pendent excess." His language suggests the autoerotic fantasy of an adolescent, self-indulgent but failing to convey, in its pompous phrasing ("pendent excess") the erotic power they hold over him. And so, he goes on at great length describing their "free state" (anticipating Naipaul's later novel, *In a Free State*), their "completeness of beauty," their painted nipples. He kisses and caresses her breasts, lays his head between them, and is grateful to Sandra for the moments she allows him to worship at this sexual shrine.

Singh's (Naipaul's?) obsession with breasts stems from a fantasy of the complete comfort and security afforded him by his mother's heavy breasts. Later in the novel he dreams he is a baby again at his mother's breasts: "What joy! The breast on my cheek and mouth: a consoling weight, the closeness of soft, smooth flesh. . . . My mother rocked and I had the freedom of her breast."

Since Sandra belongs to no community or group and has rejected her family, Singh foolishly believes that they share a common sense of alienation sufficient to hold them together. They marry and move to Isabella, where Singh sells his inherited land and begins to speculate in real estate. They become wealthy and live like aristocrats on the poor island. He feels that they have come together for self-defense against a hostile world and against their common fears. Soon, however, their marriage begins to deteriorate. They become uncomfortable when alone in the house together and they seek their happiness outside, in crowds. A feeling of failure enters their lives and they begin to sleep in separate rooms. He turns, again, to prostitutes, an experience that merely reinforces his sense of mortality: "A body which was no more than what it was, holding no promise of growth, speaking only of flesh and futility and our own imminent extinction." Finally, he realizes that Sandra has also been sleeping with other partners.

Even as his marriage was falling apart, the construction of his great new Roman house was completed. During the housewarming party, Singh's frustration vents itself in a destructive rage. The house, a symbol of wealth, marriage, and cultural roots, turns out to be a cruel parody of self-fulfillment. Singh remains a hollow man and after Sandra quietly slips out of his life, he is left with only his boyhood dream: "I have visions of Central Asian horsemen, among whom I am one, riding below a sky threatening snow to the very end of an empty world."

In the next section of the memoirs Singh goes back to the period of his childhood in Isabella hoping, perhaps, to find a lifeline to rescue him from his unfocused despair. He describes his father, a poor schoolteacher, as a fellow victim of cultural dislocation: "I used to get the feeling that my father had in some storybook way been shipwrecked on the island and that over the years the hope of rescue had altogether faded." His father was known as a "character" in Isabella. In a rage he once broke ninety-six bottles of Coca-Cola in a local shop. (His wife's wealthy family owned the bottling franchise for this prestigious soft drink). One day he abandoned his family to become a preacher in the hills, where he quickly acquired a frenzied following of the poor. Singh observes that movements like his father's "generated disorder where previously everyone had deluded himself there was order. Disorder was drama, and drama was discovered to be a necessary human nutriment."

The movement spread like fire and soon the newspapers began to take notice of it. But as Singh's later involvement in politics teaches him, disorder and drama were all his father was capable of generating: "A movement like my father's could not endure. It was . . . no more than a gesture of mass protest, a statement of despair, without a philosophy or cause." Nevertheless, his father continues to dwell in the hills for the rest of his life as an eccentric guru wearing the colorful clothes of his Hindu ancestors. When he is in London Singh sees in the newspaper a photograph of a police raid on his father's camp. Both his father and the widow with whom he was living have been shot. Singh's response to the devastating news is to pick up a whore, tell her his news, and take pleasure in her shallow sentiment and reproof. Later that night he "cried on Sandra's breasts."

Singh's father remains a shadowy figure haunting both the hills of Isabella and the paragraphs of Singh's memoirs. Although not a fully realized character, he clarifies Singh's failures. Like his father, he can only dramatize his despair, his shipwrecked condition. Later, under the influence of his former school friend, Browne, Singh exploits his father's reputation as a political and religious leader in order to win control of the political affairs of Isabella, which is at the point of independence.

One of Singh's fantasies as a boy on his derelict island is that he is the focus of some cosmic drama: "I felt . . . that I was in some way protected; a celestial camera recorded every movement, impartially, without judgment or pity. I was marked; I was of interest; I would survive." This celestial camera turns out to be none other than his own creativity demonstrated in his memoirs. He becomes his own god, so to speak, recording his least thoughts and actions with the ruthless detachment of a psychoanalytical documentary. His life is of interest and its record will assure his survival. Without his compelling fantasy as a young boy, he would be merely part of the flotsam and jetsam of the shipwreck.

The metaphor of the celestial camera was inspired by Naipaul's exposure to the popular American films that dominated the imaginative life of young Trinidadians. The film that Singh associates with his fantasy adventure into exotic lands is *The Black Swan,* a swashbuckling pirate tale starring Tyrone Power and Maureen O'Hara. The curious-looking ships and soft rippling music of the film suggest the vehicle that will transport the protected boy from Isabella to the land of mountains and snow.

One of Singh's schoolmates in Isabella was a Negro named Browne. Singh feels an Indian's sense of superiority over the island Negroes, and his visit to Browne's house creates in him a sense of violation, as if he caught his friend in a posture of indignity. On the walls of the house are pictures of Joe Louis and Haile Selassie. "I felt I had a glimpse of the prison of the spirit in which Browne lived, to which he awakened every day," Singh writes. "In those rooms he collected his facts, out of which he could make no pattern." He feels that all the attributes of Browne's race and class were secrets that no friend ought to have gazed upon. The object of this painful, introspective scene, however, is not Browne but Singh himself. As he notes, "Was it only for Browne that I was concerned?" In the last section of the novel Browne becomes Singh's political partner.

Desperate to escape from Isabella, Singh wins a scholarship to a school in London. Before he leaves he visits the home of his friend Deschampsneufs. One of the island's old French families, the Deschampsneufs consider Isabella to be paradise. They warn the young Singh that he will find this out for himself. Mr. Deschampsneufs mocks him: "I suppose you going to do like all the others and come back with a whitey-pokey." The term used by Negroes of the street people to describe white people carries an obscene connotation to Singh, but Mr. Deschampsneufs' observation proves to be not only vulgar but prophetic. The self-satisfied Deschampsneufs family proceeds to cite the beauty of the island landscape, its flora and fauna, the very sights and sounds that Singh would flee from. "All right, you go away," Mr. Deschampsneufs declares. "But you will come back. Where you born, man, you born." Indeed, Singh does return, first, literally, with Sandra (his "whitey-pokey"), and imaginatively through his memoirs. The Deschampsneufs family has seen the pattern work its way out in the lives of many other young islanders who tried to escape their desolate roots. Happy in their paradise, however, the Deschampsneufs express a smug wisdom that makes them a painful contrast to Singh's own failure and despair.

The last section of the novel, which focuses upon Singh's rise to political power in Isabella, lacks credibility. In his eagerness to depict Singh's compulsion to bring order out of the political and economic chaos that was Isabella, Naipaul ignores the realistic complexity of political ambition. Assisted by his black revolutionary friend, Browne, Singh quickly establishes a powerful socialist movement. Trading on his father's name as a radical concerned with the plight of the working class, Singh becomes an attractive public figure. Although he considers his success fraudulent, he recognizes that the popularity of his movement lies in the fact that "we offered drama." Like his father before him, Singh merely serves as a creative artist holding out the dramatic illusion of order when, in fact, society is fundamentally and irrevocably split among social, ethnic, and economic groups. As Singh observes, "In a society like ours, fragmented, inorganic, no link between man and the landscape, there was no true internal source of power, and no power was real which did not come from the outside."

It becomes clear that Singh's passionate involvement in Isabella's political life for a period of about four years is sponsored primarily by his psychological needs: "So we brought drama of a sort to the island. I will claim this as one of our achievements. Drama, however much we fear it, sharpens our perception of the world, gives us some sense of ourselves, makes us actors, gives point and sometimes glory to each day. It alters a drab landscape" (*MM*, p. 214). He goes on at great length to analyze the effect this drama had upon him: it reinforced his sense of reality, buoyed him up, and made him the chief actor within his own creation. He makes only a few cursory comments upon schools, filling stations, and shoe shops that he helped to open. Politics, like sex, other people, and writing, is chiefly there to serve Singh's profound egoism. It has no other meaning for him.

After four years of drama comes the crunch, with Singh as the appropriate sacrificial figure. The drama fails and the social chaos lying just beneath the surface of the theatrical sense of order breaks through in the form of racial unrest and a cry for nationalization to save the island's economy. Singh is sent to London in a futile attempt to salvage his deteriorating government. Refused help by the English and informed of increasing violence back home, Singh takes refuge in a sexual relationship with a young English aristrocrat named Stella. Having enjoyed several meetings with Stella in his hotel room, Singh finally becomes impotent. It was time, he says, "to leave the city of fantasy."

On his way home Singh has a stopover in northern Spain, where he picks up a prostitute. Naipaul's lengthy description of this woman's body must surely be one of the most grotesque in English literature. She is depicted as pure flesh: "She lifted herself off the bidet and sat on the bed, liquescent flesh running laterally, her breasts touching what passed for thighs. I closed my eyes and waited." The density of detail in this sexual encounter makes it possible for the narrator to disappear within this fleshy garden of forgetfulness: "The self dropped away, layer by layer; what remained dwindled to a cell of perception."

This ponderous woman comes to symbolize all of Singh's previous sexual fantasies, ranging from those of his mother's and Sandra's large breasts (the prostitute's "cascaded heavily down. They were enormous, they were grotesque") to the numerous European whores he sought in England. Here now, in Spain, he had enjoyed the mixture of horror and solace: "Through poor, hideous flesh to have learned about flesh; through flesh to have gone beyond flesh."

Naipaul's apparent abhorrence of women's bodies is thus transformed into an undefined spiritual illumination for his narrator. Singh is compelled both to seek out and to be degraded by sex, but with the Spanish whore he experienced the obliteration of time and the exquisiteness of erotic horror, and in recording the event in vivid detail he is able to rise above physical disorder and control the "striped, indented, corrugated" flesh, "the wide flabby scabbards," and "the flesh that hung in liquid folds about her legs which quivered like risen dough" within the cool, almost inhumanly detached prose of his memoirs.

In the last few pages of the novel Singh discusses his present life in the hotel and his writing. The "eighteen months of the anaesthetizing order of life in this hotel," he explains, have predisposed him to writing his memoirs. His desolate and cramped island childhood, his heroic dreams of chivalry, his formless adventures in both England and Isabella are shuffled, arranged, and rearranged at the small writing desk in a small hotel in Kensington. Thus Singh's fantasy as a child that a celestial camera was recording his every thought and move proves to be a self-fulfilling prophecy, for now the disillusioned but wiser Singh focuses his imagination upon his past and shapes a drama in which he is the melancholy hero. More significantly, however, Singh discovers an important truth at his small desk: that writing about life is not fundamentally different from life itself. As he acknowledges, "It never occurred to me that the writing of this book might have become an end in itself, that the recording of a life might become an extension of that life."

The writer in exile has learned a powerful lesson, that he must become detached, distant, analytical, self-contained, almost monkish if he is to write honestly about himself and thereby discover the buried psychological forces that previously have driven him toward repeated shipwreck. Echoing Thoreau's *Walden,* Singh observes: "We are people who for one reason or another have withdrawn, from our respective countries, from the city where we find ourselves, from our families. We have withdrawn from unnecessary responsibility and attachment. We have simplified our lives" (*MM,* p. 247). Singh believes he has at last attained an almost mystical detachment reminiscent of "damyata" (control) found in the Upanishad and quoted by Eliot in *The Waste Land.* Singh is no longer worried that at age forty he is at the end of his active life: "I no longer yearn for ideal landscapes and no longer wish to know the god of the city. . . . I have lived through attachment and freed myself from one cycle of events." Still, neither Singh nor Naipaul successfully resolve the psychological confusion, the profound sense of dislocation, and the numbing sense of failure that dominate this autobiographical fiction.

In his account of his yearlong visit to India in search of his roots, Naipaul describes the effects that his move from Trinidad to London had upon him. The details are remarkably similar to those in *The Mimic Men:*

> [London] had become the centre of my world and I had worked hard to come to it. And I was lost. London was not the centre of my world. I had been misled; but there was nowhere else to go. . . . Here I became no more than an inhabitant of a big city, robbed of loyalties, time passing, taking me away from what I was, thrown more and more into myself.[12]

Naipaul's sense of growing egotism, perhaps a defense against the impersonality of the large alien city, combined with the narrowing of his sensibilities to those of a writer rather than a man of action helped to shape the character of Ralph Singh. Like Singh, Naipaul observes that "all mythical lands faded, and in the big city I was confined to a smaller world than I had ever known. I became my flat, my desk, my name." Indeed, Naipaul makes Singh's London apartment the center of the novel. In "Writing Is Magic" he explains that he tried to write *The Mimic Men* three times before he got it going:

"The nature of the book, which is about placelessness, soon made it too diffuse. Then I realized it needed a physical centre—and this would be the place where the man was writing his memoirs. Now it appears to begin in the middle—but it couldn't be written in any other way."[13]

Within the small compass of the novel Singh explores the meaningless decades of the past and the encroaching sense of despair. Having to some extent succeeded in ordering his life through the painful creative process of writing, Singh mechanically proclaims his achievement of the fourfold division of life prescribed by his Aryan ancestors: "I have been student, householder, man of affairs, recluse." Aspects of his past life, however, he still sees as "profoundly fraudulent," especially those "in parentheses," such as his marriage to Sandra and all of the ambiguous emotions associated with that marriage. It is on the small world of the writing desk that truth appears to be most accessible: "So writing, for all its initial distortion, clarifies, and even becomes a process of life." That seems to be Singh's greatest discovery: only in the process of writing can he attain the necessary lucidity of mind with which to view himself and others.

The very last scene in the novel, however, suggests that Singh has not achieved the detachment that he earlier proclaimed. Like Caliban, he has learned the language of his master, but his identity is still unclear and his painful sense of alienation is still apparent despite the reassuring routine of his hotel life. Singh's failure is most clearly focused through his unresolved sexual compulsions and revulsion. Much excitement was created at the hotel when a special luncheon was held to honor a young but distinguished financer. The staff and permanent residents of the hotel observe the guests from the dining room. The guest of honor arrives with his wife, the Lady Stella. Recognizing her, Singh pulls his face behind a pillar and studies Garbage (his dehumanizing nickname for one of the indefatigable diners who resides at the hotel) "bringing his two-pronged knife down on the struggling cheese." Singh's deep hostility toward this socially superior white Englishwoman who raged against his impotence is clearly revealed in his fixation upon the knife about to plunge into the flesh of the cheese. Singh may no longer wish to know the god of the city because, like him, he may be a replica of Eliot's impotent fisher king.

This novel is interesting in the manner that a psychiatric case study is interesting. By adopting the cool, analytical, and dreary tone reminiscent of Robert Browning's Andrea del Sarto and Eliot's Prufrock, Naipaul runs the risk of creating a colossal bore for his narrator. John Wain's observations on this point merit quoting:

Our troubles begin when we try to feel our way toward the interior of the story. It seems to have no inside. The narrator is so little interested in the places and people he describes and so exclusively interested in himself that the book becomes oppressive. There is no escape from the confines of his personality. . . . The character we really meet is the narrator, and he, like all nimble-witted egotists, in the end becomes a bore.[14]

Ralph Singh may have offered drama to the people of Isabella and to his memories as he constructs his autobiography, but the reader unfortunately does not have many opportunities to perceive or share in that drama. Still, the narrator remains an interesting specimen of human failure, a desperate and fastidious man who creates through his memoirs an illusion of order and meaning out of the fragments of a violently disordered, absurd, and shipwrecked existence. The novel stands as Naipaul's testimony to the almost religious power of fiction to illuminate the author's secret self. In a 1968 interview Naipaul said that "at an early stage writing becomes a religious act, with the discovery and knowledge of oneself, of what one is."[15]

Ralph Singh, like his fellow Isabellans, is a mimic man whose mind and life have been twisted and controlled by the models of the West. Unlike his fellow Caribbeans, however, Singh also mimics the West in writing his memoirs. As Naipaul observes in *An Area of Darkness,* "The novel is of the West." Consequently, Indian authors who attempt to write novels violate themselves. Following Naipaul's logic, one could argue that Singh's "novel" is a degraded gesture, an elaborate egotistical fantasy given borrowed shape by the form of the English novel. Fiction may offer psychoanalytical benefits to the writer but it also corrupts the purity of thought and feeling and reinforces the despair of the hapless creator. As Singh, the hollow man, writes, "My present urge is, in the inaction imposed on me, to secure the final emptiness."

There are some other significant autobiographical themes in this novel. In a 1973 interview Naipaul explained that he had decolonized himself through writing.[16] According to John Thieme a central problem in Naipaul's thinking is his reaction to karma: "He regrets it as a paralyzing, defeatist philosophy which prevents Western-style individual self-realization and progress."[17] In *An Area of Darkness* Naipaul argues that karma lies at the heart of India's self-destructive path: "The ability to retreat, the ability genuinely not to see what was obvious" is "part of a greater philosophy of despair, leading to passivity, detachment, acceptance." He concludes with this significant observation: "It is only now, as the impatience of the observer is dissipated in the process of writing and self-inquiry, that I see how much this philosophy had also been mine." He goes on to sound remarkably like Singh: "It had enabled me to withdraw completely from nationality and loyalties except to persons; it had made me content to be myself alone, my work, my name . . .; it convinced me that every man was an island, and taught me to shield all that I knew to be good and pure within myself from the corruption of causes" (p. 198).

In a 1958 essay entitled "London," Naipaul announces that after living in London for eight years "I find I have, without effort, achieved the Buddhist ideal of non-attachment." He does not, however, feel comfortable with this achievement, for he goes on to write that "I never cease to feel that this lack of interest is all wrong. I want to be involved, to be touched even by some of the prevailing anger."[18]

Naipaul's awareness of his own Hindu sensibility and its conflict with the aggressive individualism and restlessness of the West informs his criticism of India in *An Area of Darkness,* a criticism that leads directly to *The Mimic Men,* his first novel to be written after his traumatic visit to India and his discovery in *An Area of Darkness* that he, too, is a victim of karma. John Thieme perceptively observes that in *The Mimic Men* Naipaul rejects the sterility of his hero's detachment and in so doing repudiates his [Naipaul's] own former attitude.[19] Ralph Singh, then, remains suspended in a dream world of his own making, a desperately unhappy creature who creates a comfortable cell of words and routines. Blessed with an analytical mind, capable of seeing his fatal missteps, Singh nevertheless is cursed with an egotism and defensive arrogance that make him incapable of loving another person, of caring about anyone but himself.

5

Landscapes of Fear

Naipaul's next three novels, *In a Free State, Guerrillas,* and *A Bend in the River* present an intense and chilling focus upon the elusive and paradoxical nature of freedom. All three works are set in newly independent states in Africa and the West Indies. In an atmosphere filled with racial hatred, demagogy, violence, and fear, the world of these novels produces many victims or "casualties of freedom," as Naipaul calls them. Although Naipaul maintains a style of incisive realism that reveals the brutality, fear, and homelessness of many of his characters, a fundamental romantic theme lies beneath the surface of all three novels, a theme that has been glimpsed even in his earliest stories. In the epilogue of *In a Free State,* taken from his journal, Naipaul writes: "Perhaps that had been the only pure time, at the beginning, when the ancient artist, knowing no other land, had learned to look at his own and had seen it complete." Innocence, contentment, a sense of wholeness, then, are now impossible ideals. The free state of the Edenic world is a state of mind that can now only be despairingly sought after, hoped for, perhaps occasionally felt but with the subsequent and lingering suspicion that what was felt must be an illusion.

In a Free State

In a Free State is framed by two journal entries entitled "The Tramp at Piraeus" and "The Circus at Luxor," which serve as a prologue and epilogue. After the prologue there are two stories, "One out of Many" and "Tell Me Who to Kill," followed by the short novel that gives the volume its title. Although these several pieces are not connected by their characters or setting and could not properly be considered sections of a single, unified novel, they are nevertheless thematically relevant to the title novella and one assumes that Naipaul arranged them for that purpose.

In "The Tramp at Piraeus" Naipaul describes a sadistic attack upon a tramp that he witnessed during a trip he took on a Greek steamer from Piraeus to Alexandria. The dingy vessel is a microcosm of the homeless. Its passengers are made up of Italians, Americans, Lebanese, and Egyptian Greeks ("Egypt was no longer their home. They had been expelled; they were refugees"). Naipaul goes on to say that after the invaders left Egypt and after many humiliations, Egypt was free but that these poor Greeks, who were only just less poor than the Egyptians, "were the casualties of that freedom." In both his earlier and later works, Naipaul continues to emphasize this point with regards to the Third World nations—the Africans and the West Indians, for example, whose lives are uprooted and manipulated by the futile ambitions of their rulers, who are corrupted by the forces of Western democracy.

The tramp, who appears to be English, is a mysterious, small old man who claims to have traveled all over the world. He therefore proclaims himself "a citizen of the world." He looks for company, wants to be noticed, but at the same time he appears to want solitude. Naipaul becomes fascinated with this figure, especially since his presence becomes the focus of the other passengers. A Lebanese businessman, infuriated that the tramp slept in one of the bunks in their small cabin, swears that he will kill him. Enlisting the help of a powerful Austrian teenager, the Lebanese proceeds to attack the old man but he eventually manages to escape their violence and locks himself in one of the lavatories. Knowing his life is in danger, he later locks himself in the cabin for the duration of the voyage, threatening to set it on fire if anyone dares to enter. As the ship finally docks and the passengers move down the gangplank, the tramp successfully makes his exit. The Austrian boy sees him but takes no real interest in him at this point. The Lebanese, who enjoyed a restful night, did not even see the tramp leave the ship. As Naipaul simply reports, "That passion was over."

This simple narrative sets the tone and theme of the stories and short novel to follow. The tramp's boast that he is not bound by national constraints, that he is "a citizen of the world," suggests that he possesses a freedom not available to the other passengers, who stay within their national factions. The cramped quarters aboard ship exacerbate the tension between national boundaries, and the easiest way for the Arabs to release their tension is to find a scapegoat. Small, vulnerable, different, the tramp becomes the object of their hostility. The citizen of the world, ironically, makes his escape and secures his freedom by locking himself within a toilet and then a cabin. The attempt to find the enemy, kill him, and thereby attain, if not a solution to one's frustrations and rage, at least a release of a crippling passion, can be traced throughout this book and the next. The potential violence of the Arab and Austrian in this prologue culminates in *Guerrillas*, where the West Indian, Jimmy Ahmed, sodomizes Jane, a white Englishwoman, before taking her to his homosexual lover, who hacks her to death with a sword.

The narrator of "One out of Many" is an Indian named Santosh. He introduces himself: "I am now an American citizen and I live in Washington, capital of the world. Many people, both here and in India, will feel that I have done well. But." The rest of the story hangs on that last word, for Santosh has come to discover the paradox of freedom: in seeking it he has lost it. As he says, "I was so happy in Bombay. I was respected. I had a certain position." Unlike the ancient artist that Naipaul describes in the epilogue, Santosh has sacrificed his pure state in leaving Bombay, where he was whole and content, and having come to America, he can no longer see either his homeland or America the same way again, and neither they nor he can ever be complete. His new experience and knowledge have devastated his innocence.

Santosh, a servant for an Indian in government service, suddenly finds his world in an upheaval when his employer informs him that he has been posted to Washington. Feeling that he cannot return to his village life, Santosh pleads with his employer to take him along. His dream of a new and free adventure is quickly darkened by the trip itself. Santosh becomes terribly sick on the plane and vomits all over his bundles. The constraints on his dream continue, as his employer moves into a spacious apartment and Santosh is relegated to a small closet. Since his servile attitude limits his expectations, he finds the accommodations completely to his liking. As his experiences develop and his horizons grow, however, Santosh finds himself more and more a prisoner in a free land.

Santosh's glimpse of America does not seem real. In television commercials he sees the Americans whom in real life he seldom saw. The American Hare Krishnas baffle him with their bad Sanskrit pronunciation and their accent. His attempt to understand who they are leads him to reflect Naipaul's own sense of Indian estrangement in Trinidad. Santosh thinks that these people were now strangers, but that perhaps once upon a time they had been like him: "Perhaps, as in some story, they had been brought here among the *hubshi* [blacks] as captives a long time ago and had become a lost people, like our own wandering gypsy folk, and had forgotten who they were." In any event, Santosh early on comes to accept the fact that he is a prisoner. "I accepted this and adjusted," he says.

When he discovers that a black maid at the apartment finds him attractive, he begins to change his attitude toward himself. "Now I found that, without wishing it, I was ceasing to see myself as part of my employer's presence," he says. His growing assertion of his individuality then gets confused with his sexual desires, his sense of guilt, and his longing for self destruction. Wanting to be cleansed after his sexual encounter with the maid, Santosh discovers that the blacks have rioted and set fire to sections of Washington. Santosh explains that he wanted the fire to spread throughout the city and destroy everything in its path, "even the apartments, even myself, to be destroyed and consumed. I wanted escape to be impossible; I wanted the very idea of escape to become absurd."

Although the fire does not fulfill Santosh's wish, his growing involvement within his limited Washington world does. By the end of the story he discovers that the idea of escape and of freedom is absurd. Ashamed of his actions with the maid and fearful of her continued presence, he becomes a chef at an Indian restaurant. Circumstances continue to imprison him. He is afraid to walk the street lest he run into his employer, whom he has abandoned, or the black maid. Furthermore, he has to hide from his new employer the fact that he does not have a working permit. Burdened by his secrets and terrified by the responsibility that for the first time he has taken for his own life he "saw the future as a hole into which I was dropping." Like Mr. Biswas, he has suffered the dreadful vision of the void.

Santosh ponders his paradoxical state: "I was good-looking; I had lost my looks. I was a free man; I had lost my freedom." He beguiles himself with the same false consolation of karma as did Ralph Singh in *The Mimic Men* when he thinks, "To be empty is not to be sad. To be empty is to be calm. It is to renounce."

Santosh finally compromises and settles for a life somewhere between detachment and involvement. He marries the black maid, thereby becoming a citizen, and continues to work as a chef. On the other hand, he closes his mind and heart to the English language and refuses to watch television or listen to the radio. "I do not want to understand or learn any more," he says. Unable to return to the childlike innocence of his past in Bombay, at least he can limit his present experiences and knowledge in the hope that he will not further fragment his damaged identity. His final observations are incisive and reflect Naipaul's troubling understanding of freedom as a deadly force:

> I was once part of the flow, never thinking of myself as a presence. Then I looked into the mirror and decided to be free. All that my freedom has brought me is the knowledge that I have a face and have a body, that I must feed and clothe this body for a certain number of years. Then it will be over.[1]

Santosh finally gets his wish, sponsored earlier by his overwhelming sense of guilt, that the very idea of escape becomes absurd.

The narrator of "Tell Me Who to Kill" is a Trinidadian who, while en route to his brother's wedding in England, reveals through his interior monologue a terrifying madness and potential for violence. His early memories of growing up in the dreary and hopeless atmosphere of Trinidad help to reinforce his obsession to help his younger brother, Dayo, to escape from the poverty and cultural imprisonment of his island world. Fantasy and reality, however, constantly blend and reveal the narrator's tenuous grasp on his sanity. Raised in poverty and nourished by American films, he tends to see people and events in terms of the cinema fantasy. He hopes that Dayo will grow up to look like "Errol Flim" or "Fairley Granger" and later, when he is grown, notes that he walks like Henry Fonda. With the continued allusions to Hollywood films it soon becomes clear that the narrator is not using them to be picturesque but that he cannot separate fact from fiction.

He explains how hard he worked to support his brother in his studies only to learn that his brother was lazy, a liar, and simply did not want the life being shaped for him. He drops out of school, gets a job, and decides to marry a white woman. The narrator has no life of his own. As he explains, locked up in his mind is the burning awareness that his world is without hope, "with nothing good in it, nothing to see except surgarcane and the pitch road, and how from small I know I had no life." And so, he lives simply to help his brother and when he fails at that, the narrator's inner rage and hatred seek a victim and can find none. During the wedding dinner he thinks:

> They take my money, they spoil my life, they separate us. But you can't kill them. O God, show me the enemy. Once you find out who the enemy is, you can kill him. But these people here they confuse me. . . . My brother was to be the educated one, the nice one. And this is how it is ending, in this room, eating with these people. Tell me who to kill. (pp. 101–2).

Unlike the Lebanese in "The Tramp at Piraeus," the mad narrator here is at least sane enough to realize that he cannot single out any one person or group to blame for his lifelong misery and frustration. His cry, "Tell me who to kill," is terrible in proportion to its being unanswerable.

Naipaul describes *In a Free State* as "a very, very hard book to write. There is dialogue all the way through, and for that to work you have to establish the lives and relationships of all the people precisely. But you also have to get what is happening outside. Even the history of the land plays an important part."[2] Naipaul feels justifiably proud that his novel captured a political reality that anticipated the social upheavals in Uganda in the 1970s. "I began to write the book in '69," he writes, "before anyone can have seen exactly how accurate my predictions would be. I got a fabulous roasting when the book came out in 1971. Our African 'man' hadn't really shown his hand then. The book offended a lot of people who just couldn't visualize these developments in a land like Uganda, which I drew with touches of Kenya and one or two other countries."[3]

Years later, however, Naipaul came to realize that despite the African setting and the white English characters who are the focus of the novel, this book was actually about himself. After having settled in England for several years trying to establish himself as a writer, Naipaul decided to sell his home and travel throughout the West Indies. Having spent two years researching and writing *The Loss of El Dorado,* he relished the idea of being free to roam. When he arrived in the United States he discovered that his Boston publisher really wanted a popular book for tourists, not a critical analysis of Trinidad. Profoundly depressed and angry, and lacking the cash advance he had assumed the book would bring, he made his way back to England. His journey seemed to him now to be a caricature of his first traumatic trip from his island region. "It was out of this grief, too deep for tears or rage," he writes, "that I began to write my African story, which had come to me as a wisp of an idea in Africa three or four years before." In the quiet village of Wiltshire, where Naipaul started up his new life in England, he began to transpose his sense of menace and fear from the pastoral countryside to Africa.

Africa had given his white hero and heroine "a chance, made them bigger, brought out their potential; now, when they were no longer so young, it was consuming them." It is a book about fear, Naipaul says:

> All the jokes were silenced by this fear. And the mist that hung over the valley where I was writing; the darkness that came early; the absence of knowledge of where I was—all this uncertainty emanating from the valley I transferred to my Africa.[4]

Uprooted, alien, and fearful, Naipaul unwittingly became the subject of his novel. Later, in *The Enigma of Arrival,* he acknowledges this realization as he discovers that all of his fiction, insofar as it is honest, is a disclosure of aspects of his life. In the case of the present novel, he continues, "The African fear with which as a writer I was living day after day; the unknown Wiltshire; the cruelty of this return to England, the dread of a second failure; the mental fatigue. All this, rolled into one, was what lay on the spirit of the man who went on the walks down to Jack's cottage and past it" (pp. 102–3).

Naipaul ironically opens his novel in the manner of a fairy tale or a fable: "In this country in Africa there was a president and there was also a king." Although the story that follows embodies both a psychological and political realism, the fairy-tale opening prepares the reader for the depressing and incisive customary moral of such a tale, a moral applicable to many of the emerging Third World nations, namely, that political independence is limited, dangerous, and destructive. The imposition of Western ideas and ambitions upon a nation with ancient tribal loyalties and traditions brings about not liberation but hatred, distrust, frustration, violence, and slavery.

Set in East Africa at the time of a coup reminiscent of the Uganda State of Emergency of 1966, the story begins at the point where the president, supported by white governments, has just sent out his powerful army against the king's people. Naipaul focuses his narrative upon the effect that this dangerous political unrest has upon his two main characters—Bobby and Linda—during their two-day, four hundred mile drive, from the capital to the compound where they are employed in the Southern Collectorate.

Bobby, an administrative officer in the central government, is an Englishman, a homosexual who has come to Africa to indulge his sadomasochistic passion. In England his homosexuality led to disgrace, which is one of the reasons that brought him to this land, where he can enjoy the freedom of sexual liaisons with young black men. He relishes the power he holds over the Africans and at the same time desires to be punished by them. "You do terrible things," he confides to Linda, "to prove to yourself that you are a real person." Bobby's character is further complicated by his sentimental and romantic image of Africa. Having suffered a nervous breakdown at Oxford, he now beckons Linda, as the two of them drive through picturesque East Africa, to "look at that lovely tree," adding, "Africa saved my life." Naipaul interprets the remark "as though [Bobby] was at once punishing and forgiving all who misunderstood him." Several times Bobby exclaims, "My life is here." His self-conscious dress—he calls attention to his African shirt—further underscores his false, selfish, and shallow identification with the natives.

Linda is a white Englishwoman, married to one of the officials in the Collectorate. When Bobby is asked to give her a lift back to the compound, he is annoyed: "Africa was for Bobby the empty spaces, the safe adventure of long fatiguing drives on open roads, the other Africans, boys built like men." To make matters worse, Linda is an unattractive woman showing her age. In the Collectorate compound she has the reputation as a man-eater. During the long drive to their safe quarters Linda's presence elicits Bobby's fears, dreams, and hostility. Unlike Bobby, who enjoys nourishing his romantic illusions about Africa, Linda adopts the prejudices and superiority of the colonial European toward the country. She admits that she and her husband made a mistake when they first came to Africa: "We should have taken our courage in both hands and gone back home." Later she says, "I hated this place from the first day I came here. . . . I felt I had no right to be among these people." Although neither Bobby nor Linda has a critical understanding of this alien world, Linda at least sees more clearly than Bobby the menace and brutal reality that begin to envelop them during their last ride together.

In Naipaul's description of the capital, where Bobby and Linda are attending a seminar on community development, he establishes the fundamental cultural duality that encompasses the entire novel. The capital, the reader is told, was "an English–Indian creation in the African wilderness." Owing nothing to African skill, the capital is filled with tourist shops displaying souvenir carvings, leather goods, drums, and spears. "Africa here was decor," Naipaul writes, "a colonial city, with a colonial glamour. Everyone in it was far from home." Even the African himself, "flushed out from the bush," was an alien here. The immediate conflict may be between the president and the king's people, but the ultimate polarity is between the Westernized Africa—obsessed with power, violence, and reformation—and the Africa of the bush, which possesses a long history and a cultural integrity.

Throughout the novel Linda and Bobby share glimpses of a mysterious, private, and ancient world that they can never understand with their accustomed Western perceptions, and this world, consequently, becomes as menacing to them as does the actual brutal encounters they have with the president's militia. At one time Linda sees some natives along the road whose bodies are covered with white chalk, and later sees a group of Africans in bright clothes, walking in the rain, covering their heads with leaves so that they were nearly impossible to see against the trees. She says to Bobby,

"That's the sort of thing that makes me feel far from home. I feel that sort of forest life has been going on forever." The hillside along which Bobby and Linda are driving suddenly becomes alive with Africans, and Linda says, "You could disappear here without a trace." As Angus Calder observes, no other writer since Conrad has "exposed the otherness of Africa so starkly, and Naipaul leaves his readers freer by his massacre of obstinate illusions."[5]

One of Naipaul's great achievements in this novel is his creation of the devastating sense of menace and terror that lie beneath the surface of seemingly ordinary experiences. As Bobby and Linda begin their trip to the compound they hear the violent "yak yak yak yak" of a helicopter hovering above them. The president's men keep a suspicious and watchful eye upon the two outsiders, but it is only later, well into their trip, that Bobby and Linda come to realize just how dangerous their situation is. Their car ride itself is perceived as perilous, for as Linda observes, "Nearly everybody you meet had been in an accident or knew someone who had been in an accident." Later on a military truck tries to run them off the road and they luckily escape harm.

Naipaul contrasts the natural beauty of Africa with frequent images of ugly, derelict buildings and outposts along the road. Coming to one such devastated and straggling settlement, Linda sees a crowd of Africans walking along the road and jokingly remarks, "They are restless today." The black, featureless faces stare unnervingly into the car, making Linda's old joke seem ironically serious. "I must say I didn't like the looks we got there," Bobby remarks. Even the weather begins to turn ominous. Bobby observes the sky and says, "I don't like the way those clouds are piling up there." And so they decide to make a stop at the Hunting Lodge, seemingly a safe harbor in the coming storm.

One of the recurrent images in the novel is that of the president's photograph, which hangs prominently in most establishments, including the Hunting Lodge. Like a sinister Big Brother, he looks out of various frames upon Bobby and Linda wherever they go, and his power can be felt in the mysterious Africans who seem to appear out of nowhere to cast a threatening shadow upon the two of them. When they enter the lodge Bobby sees an African and Naipaul simply observes that "the African was smiling." But it is the sinister smile of a deadly Cheshire Cat. Throughout their brief stopover the African continues to gaze at them, smiling, standing off by himself in silence. When they finally prepare to leave they are asked to give the African a lift. Identifying himself simply as a trade unionist, he suddenly tells Bobby to stop the car to pick up another African, his friend. When they insist that they be driven in a direction other than the one Bobby intends, Linda, no longer able to restrain her prejudice and anger, opens the car door and makes them leave. "What a smell!" she exclaims, "Absolute gangsters. I'm not going to get myself killed simply because I'm too nice to be rude to Africans." Bobby acknowledges that the first African's presence at the lodge was sinister, and now, looking into his rear view mirror, he sees the two men walking back toward the lodge, rather than in the direction that they claimed they wanted to go.

The scene where Bobby and Linda stop at a filling station in Esher gives the first clear indication of Bobby's own violent nature. Despite his sentimentality and romanticism, in moments of stress he exhibits the colonial spirit of arrogance, superiority, and brutality. When one of the native service station attendants ignorantly scratches Bobby's windshield while attempting to clean it, Bobby flies into a rage and knocks the man to the ground with his car door. When the African turns his back on him Bobby is about to strike him but Linda rather calmly intervenes and keeps the situation from getting out of hand.

Their next adventure is more bizarre and displays an aspect of Naipaul's recurrent fascination with an abhorrence of female sexuality. Linda gets stung on her rump by a bee, gets out of the car and attempts to examine herself. Bobby studies the body that she displays: "the thin yellow folds of the moist skin, the fragile ribs, the brassiere, put on for the day's adventure, enclosing those poor little breasts, and below the waistband of her blue trousers the undergarments that looked as strapped and surgical as the brassiere." In a melodramatic gesture Bobby leans over and kisses the red bump, after which he tells her that he hopes she does not misinterpret his intention. Naipaul's obsession with women who possess full, pendulous breasts contrasts sharply with this Englishwoman's sexual poverty. The references to the yellow skin, the strapped and surgical undergarment and brassiere all contribute to the unpleasant image of her sexuality.

Later in the novel Naipaul reveals that Bobby's foolish and sentimental response after Linda got stung was mere empty drama. Much more real is his powerful hatred, born in part from his own wounded sexuality and in part from his recognition of Linda's somewhat keener perception of the menace that continues to grow around them, a menace that threatens Bobby's small and selfish world of fantasy. While spending the night at a hotel in a derelict colonial town Bobby looks through Linda's room while she is downstairs and discovers among her rumpled clothes "a vaginal deodorant with an appalling name. The slut, Bobby thought, the slut. . . . Bobby was hating everything." Hours later, when they are back on the road, Linda begins to rail against the Africans: "You should either stay away, or you should go among them with the whip in your hand. Anything in between is ridiculous." (This image of the whip becomes the central metaphor for the epilogue, to be discussed next). Bobby responds with bitter sarcasm: "We are among these very dirty savages and we must remind ourselves that we have this loveliness. Do we use our vaginal deodorant daily?" He then dehumanizes her by attacking her sexuality: "You're nothing. You're nothing but a rotting cunt. There are millions like you, millions, and there will be millions more." Female sexuality is mere carrion, made more repulsive by the attempt to sweeten it with deodorant sprays. In his next two novels, *Guerrillas* and *A Bend in the River,* Naipaul once again has his protagonists take out their hatred and frustrations upon female sexuality. In these two works the images of rotting flesh, spittle, feces, rape, and sadistic murder are grotesquely combined with the sexuality of white women.

Bobby seeks a world that will safely cater to his homosexual and selfish needs, a world that he has fashioned to be both romantic and antiseptic. During his mental breakdown in England, he confesses to Linda, he always consoled himself "with the fantasy of driving through a cold and rainy night endless miles, until I came to a cottage right at the top of a hill. There would be a fire there, and it would be warm and I would be perfectly safe." In his fantasy he further imagines that everything in the warm room is "absolutely white," white curtains in the breeze, white walls, and a white bed. The world he inhabits now, however, as Linda constantly reminds him, is black, sinister, hot, and dangerous. Even the compound, to which they are heading, cannot afford perfect safety.

When Linda tells him that she feels that the forest life around them has been going on forever, Bobby replies, "You've been reading too much Conrad. I hate that book, don't you?" Naipaul's own fascination with Conrad comes to the surface here, suggesting a loose comparison between Bobby and Linda's drive through Africa with that of Marlowe's voyage into the heart of darkness. Although Naipaul's characters are too shallow to experience or understand the horrific and dehumanizing encounter of a Marlowe with Mr. Kurtz, they nevertheless have to come to grips with their own illusions about themselves and their surroundings by the end of their journey. The veneer of civilized decorum gradually breaks away as they move deeper into a terrifying and derelict Africa they never imagined.

In the episode where Bobby and Linda stop over at the Colonel's run-down hotel, a relic of better colonial times, Naipaul creates a powerful sense of impending disaster for the old order. The Colonel is like a lion-tamer, who, though he has his bush African employees under control for the moment, knows they are just waiting for their chance to attack and kill him. The hatred of these men, he acknowledges, keeps him alert and alive. The Colonel is a fatalist, who knows he will be murdered by these people. He says, "They say there's good and bad everywhere. There's no good and bad here. They're just Africans. They do what they have to do." Unlike Bobby and Linda, the Colonel has no illusions about Africa, recognizes the failure of European attempts to reshape it (his very hotel with its decadent furnishings is a veritable microcosm of that failure), and has matter-of-factly accepted his impending murder as inevitable.

The atmosphere around the hotel becomes surrealistically terrifying as Bobby and Linda walk outside at night and encounter a pack of dogs. Brought here years earlier to attack Africans, they have now become feral and threateningly roam the area. Once again Bobby's thinly disguised civility is undercut: "I'll kill them. I'm wearing these steel-tipped shoes. I'll kill the first one that attacks me. I'll kick its skull in. I'll kill it." The developing sense of fear and violence continues when one of the African employees that Bobby tried to seduce with money earlier in the day comes to his room later that night to collect and stands over his bed: "Sitting up in bed, looking at the inflamed African face coming nearer to his, he saw it invaded by such blank and mindless rage that his own anger vanished in terror, terror at something he sensed to be beyond his control, beyond his reason." This young man, "fresh from the bush," is just another of many examples of Bobby's grotesque inability to interpret the world around him. Behind the colonial dream and reasoned order of things lie a primitive chaos and rage, and the impenetrable enigma of Africa.

As Bobby and Linda drive away from the Colonel's hotel, she remarks that the foolish old man is trying to live on his will alone: "He wanted the company. And he's right. They're waiting to kill him." Bobby rationalizes the situation by saying that the Colonel could go south if he wanted to: "Still a lot of blacks there he can take it out of." At this point in their journey they have at least come to the understanding that they must look after themselves first and foremost and quickly abandon their concern for the Colonel. As Linda says, "I suppose you're right. Let the dead bury the dead." What they do not appear to understand, however, in their growing cynicism, is that they themselves are hollow people whose diminished humanity has been highlighted by their recent experiences.

Toward the end of their drive Bobby and Linda come across the president's military with a group of helpless prisoners who do not seem to understand their terrible fate. Sitting on the ground, some are prostrate and most are naked: "They were slender, small-boned, very black people of the king's tribe, a clothed people, builders of roads. But such dignity as they had possessed in freedom had already gone; they were only forest people now, in the hands of their enemies." Some are tied up "in the traditional forest way," all show marks of having been beaten, and a few look dead. Here are the graphic consequences of the progressive new state. The members of the military cruelly mimic their colonial invaders (though still retaining some of their bush techniques) and in so doing destroy both the dignity and freedom of their own native people.

Bobby attempts to impress the soldiers by telling them that his "boss-man" is an African and that he has to be back at the Collectorate before the curfew. A fat soldier, interested merely in Bobby's watch, begins to toy with him and then throws him to the ground and bangs his head against the floor. Knowing he will be killed if he does not do something, Bobby recalls Linda's advice that when one runs into the military he should play dead. Bobby survives the encounter, but his beating, partially brought about by his own inept handling of a dangerous situation, has its roots in his own sadomasochistic personality. The same arrogance and violence exhibited by the fat soldier lie within Bobby's own character, as evidenced by his near attack upon the service station attendant at Esher and by his subsequent treatment of his servant at the Collectorate.

One of the last images of Africa that Bobby and Linda have as they escape with their lives and head, finally, toward their compound, is that of the burning of the king's villages. "They were a people," Naipaul writes, "who lived, vulnerably now, in villages along their ancient straight roads: roads that had spread their power as forest conquerors, until the first explorers came." Their ancient world has been undermined by the white explorers and their proud children now lie roped like animals by the president's men, who plunder and burn their homes. Even the appearance of these ancient peoples has been corrupted. Women and children, returning to the ruins of the villages, looked "over-dressed in their Edwardian costumes."

When Bobby and Linda finally return to the safety of their compound Linda is free of her panic: "The compound was her setting; she had news." Presumably, she will revert to her normal routine and return to England as soon as possible. Bobby, on the other hand, has learned little from his previous experiences; rather, his imperial attitude has intensified. He discovers that his African servant, Luke, has been drinking in his absence. He thinks: "I will have to leave. But the compound was safe; the soldiers guarded the gate. Bobby thought: I will have to sack Luke." The novella ends with this reflection, an observation that captures the essence of Bobby's sadistic, exploitative character. In an amazing twist of priorities, Bobby allows his sense of superiority over Luke to displace his first thought, that of leaving Africa. The fact that Luke is one of the king's tribe and that he drinks and attends a Christian church contributes to Bobby's sense of the man's debased Africanism. In planning to sack him Bobby embodies the same cruelty as the military who burn the villages and torture the bush Africans. Victim and victimizer, Bobby has driven into the heart of darkness and has become an integral part of its corruption.

In his "Epilogue, from a Journal," Naipaul records an incident of cruelty that he witnessed at a tourist hotel in Luxor, Egypt. Sitting on a terrace at a table with two Germans, Naipaul watches as an Egyptian, with a camel whip at his waist, moves among the tables serving coffee. Naipaul then notices a group of desert children on the fringe of the terrace and a cruel game begins to take shape. A group of Italians "as they understood the rules of the game, became playful." They throw out pieces of their sandwiches onto the sand and when the children come to pick them up the Egyptian shouts at the children and strikes them with his whip. As the game continues the various national groups—English, American, and German—pay no attention. "Lucidity, and anxiety," Naipaul writes, "came to me only when I was almost on the man with the camel-whip. I was shouting. I took the whip away, threw it on the sand." The Egyptian, to make amends, offers him some free coffee, but Naipaul, knowing the desert children would soon return to gather up the scraps of food, leaves the terrace and continues on his journey. Reflecting on the various empires that had come and gone in the area, and now, with another more remote empire announcing itself, Naipaul thinks that "all that was asked in return was anger and a sense of injustice." It is within this context that he concludes that perhaps the only pure time existed "at the beginning, when the ancient artist, knowing no other land, had learned to look at his own and had seen it as complete."

By taking the whip from the Egyptian, then, Naipaul suggests a temporary stay against the confusion, violence, and injustice that pervade the lives of all the characters of *In a Free State*. A small gesture in an absurd world, the removal of the whip from the tormentor is a significant dramatic action for Naipaul who, up to this point, has chosen to remain a detached recorder of the irony, suffering, and dehumanization of his characters. The anger and sense of injustice that may have prompted this symbolic action, however, do not mark a clear turning point in Naipaul's fiction, for *Guerrillas*, his next novel, presents an even bleaker image of humanity's hopelessness. Nevertheless, one cannot help but feel that in his strong identification with the desert children, Naipaul finds an analogy with his own mental state at the time. Having failed in *The Loss of El Dorado* to please his publisher and having only recently returned to England to begin anew his attempt to succeed as a writer, Naipaul saw himself as an alien, working on the edge of a culture he fantasized about but to which he was barred by circumstance and birth. The psychological whip that kept him back and worked its cruel injustice upon his dreams can be controlled and put down, at least for a while.

Guerrillas

From 1970 to 1973 Naipaul experienced a "creative gap." Unable to write fiction, he turned instead to writing several extended essays, including such subjects as Michael X, a black revolutionist from Trinidad, the new Peronism, Mobutu's new "authentic Africa," and Conrad's vision of South America, Africa, and the Far East. Published in the London *Times* in 1973, two years before the appearance of *Guerrillas,* "Michael X and the Black Power Killings in Trinidad" is an intense and obsessional account of hatred, cant, black-power jargon, and murder that served as the basis for Naipaul's next novel. This long essay is perhaps the best introduction to *Guerrillas.*

Michael de Freitas, also known as Michael X and Michael Abdul Malik, was the son of a Portuguese shopkeeper and an uneducated black woman from Barbados. A "red man" who "passed" when it was convenient to his rise to power, he only became black when he arrived in London from Trinidad. Malik had spent fourteen years in England, having arrived in 1957 as a Trinidadian seaman named Michael de Frietas, aged twenty-four. He lived in Notting Hill where he became a pimp, drug dealer, and gambling-house operator. He underwent a religious-political conversion and chose the name Michael X. Within ten years of his arrival in England he became a notorious black power leader and writer. He was then jailed for a year for an antiwhite speech. Upon his release, he founded his first commune, the Black House, in Islington. The "urban village" failed, however, and in 1971, under the name Michael Abdul Malik, he fled to Trinidad.

In Trinidad he opened another commune, called Christina Gardens, a would-be revolutionary center that purported to be an agricultural commune. In 1972 two visitors showed up at Christina Gardens, an American black power leader named Hakim Jamal and his worshiping mistress, Gale Ann Benson, a twenty-seven-year-old middle-class English divorcee. She believed that Jamal was god. The people who knew her detected a madness and fakery about her. She took the name Hale Kimga, an anagram of Gale and Hakim, and wore elaborate African-style clothes. Naipaul observes: "The absurd cult, the absurd name, the absurd clothes—everything that is remembered of Benson in Trinidad suggests the great uneducated vanity of the middle-class dropout."

Malik and his cohorts, in their paranoia, came to suspect that she was a secret agent of British intelligence and planned her murder. A hole was dug in the area of a dunghill for her body and several men pulled her into the hole where they repeatedly slashed her body with a cutlass. Covered with wounds but her feet still kicking, she was buried in four feet of manure and left to suffocate. Naipaul describes this horrific act in great detail with an objectivity that makes the murder blindingly painful to witness.

In *Guerrillas* Naipaul has the character based upon Benson sodomized before being slashed to death. While the deaths of Benson and her fictional counterpart, Jane, acknowledge the madness of the half-breed revolutionaries, they also seem to be a punishment for fakery. Naipaul writes that "Benson was, more profoundly than Malik or Jamal, a fake. She took, on her journey away from home, the assumptions, however little acknowledged, not only of her class and race and the rich countries to which she belonged, but also of her ultimate security." This observation applies not only to Benson and Jane, but to Bobby and Linda in *In a Free State*.

Malik's image of himself was always way out of proportion to his actual importance. Having achieved fame, friends, and money in England, he foolishly considered himself one of the greatest black leaders of his time and in a failed ghosted autobiography proclaims his successes and fantasies. In England there were people who convinced him that he was a writer, a poet and, under the influence of marijuana, he would write incoherent pages that blended fact with fiction. As Naipaul observes, "With words he remade his past; words also gave him a pattern for the future." Like Jimmy Ahmed, his counterpart in *Guerrillas*, Malik's fictional fantasies became his reality and his undoing.

About the same time that Benson was murdered, Malik personally slaughtered with his cutlass another person, a man named Joe

Skerritt. When the bodies of Skerritt and Benson were discovered the police tracked down Malik and his handful of conspirators. Malik was hanged in Port of Spain about three and a half years after the death of Benson. According to Naipaul the people of Trinidad had come to recognize Malik as a " 'character,' a Carnival figure, a dummy Judas to be beaten through the streets on Good Friday." Naipaul argues that even in London and in the halcyon days of his newspaper fame as Michael X, Malik was the same carnival figure: "the militant who was only an entertainer, the leader who had no followers, the Black Power man who was neither powerful nor black. He wasn't even black; he was 'a fair-skin man,' half white. That, in the Trinidad phrase, was the sweetest part of the joke."

In *Guerrillas* Naipaul transforms the character of Malik into Jimmy Ahmed, half-Chinese, half-black, who has recently been deported from England, where he established his credentials as a black militant, to an unnamed West Indian island where he sets up an "agricultural" commune called Thrushcross Grange. Ahmed takes the name for his commune from *Wuthering Heights*, a book he was required to read in a writing course. Like Malik, Ahmed considers himself a writer and during the course of the novel Naipaul weaves into the narrative several pages of Ahmed's rambling, violent writings.

The other central characters are Roche and Jane who, in an opening scene reminiscent of Bobby and Linda in *In a Free State*, are driving together toward Ahmed's commune. Roche is a white liberal who has won considerable notice for a book about his experiences in South Africa, where he was arrested, tortured, tried, and imprisoned for his beliefs. Finally, he was deported and came to work in the West Indies in the hope of promoting humanitarian causes. Jane, like Benson, is an English divorcee, now living with Roche. Seeking an adventure after her divorce, Jane is impressed by Roche because he seems to be a doer, a man who suffers greatly for his convictions. Her romanticism quickly betrays her, however, and she finds Roche lacking in passion and too keen to direct sarcasm her way. She imagined that he would remake her world, but instead she finds after four months what she has suspected from the beginning: "that she had come to a place at the end of the world, to a place that had exhausted its possibilities."

Clearly the grimmest and most cynical of all Naipaul's novels, *Guerrillas* opens with a series of long descriptive passages of the countryside as Roche and Jane drive toward the Grange, passages filled with images of decay and ruin that foreshadow the death and destruction to come and that suggest the spiritual emptiness of the major characters themselves. The texture of the countryside is comprised of swampy odors, bauxite dust, burning rubbish, rusting cars, wire fences, and concrete ruins. In the commune they find a junked typewriter, junked duplicator, some metal trays, and outside they see desolation everywhere and smell the feces and urine from a nearby corrugated iron latrine. Jane reflects upon her dream that Roche was going to enlarge her vision of the world.

In these early chapters Naipaul describes Jane over and over again as someone remarkably like Benson—privileged because she is secure. She has a return ticket to England and, unlike the people around her, she can escape whenever she wants to. "She had always seen decay about her," Naipaul writes. "Security was the basis of her privilege." "Out of this knowledge of her own security," he continues, "and her vision of decay, of a world running down, she moved from one crisis to another." Ironically, her sense of security, like that of Benson, proves to be her fatal flaw.

In an interview given in 1981 Naipaul commented on his novel: "It has very hard things to say about people who play at serious things, who think they can always escape, run back to their safe world. The woman in the novel is a study in vanity."[6] Be that as may, her treatment seems to reflect Naipaul's own sexual hostility and his profound jealousy of the European's sense of place and security. Even the narrator of "Tell Me Who to Kill," angry and frustrated to the point of committing murder, echoes Naipaul's jealousy as he observes the tourists in London: "But these people come for the day; they are happy, they have buses to take them back to their hotels; they have countries to go back to, they have houses. The sadness I feel make my heart seize" (*IFS*, p. 94).

Naipaul depicts Jimmy Ahmed as a small, taut, trimly dressed man whose exterior sense of self-control masks a profound rage and hatred. In his maniacal egotism, he convinces himself that only he stands between social order and chaos on the island, that all of the capitalists support him in order to secure their investments against a threatened revolution. Although Naipaul only hints at Malik's bisexuality—a boy named Parmassar stays with him—he portrays Ahmed as a bisexual enjoying the favors of Bryant, a sullen and aggressive young black who lives in the commune.

It becomes clear, even in the early sections of the novel, that Ahmed's sexuality is a complex expression of his hatred and his sense of rejection. Enjoying the thrill of another adventure, Jane allows herself to be lured to Ahmed's house the day after her arrival. Naipaul describes their first sexual encounter as a rather sordid affair. Jane's language, her manipulative manner, the descriptions of the stain on the bed, the perspiration, the ugly details of her and Ahmed's bodies, and Roche's phone call just before the sex act all contribute to an antierotic scene. Explaining, "I'm not good," Ahmed is humiliated by a weak premature ejaculation: "Without convulsions, his little strength leaked out of him, and it was all over. And he raged inside." Jane dresses and becomes almost a stranger again and Ahmed's hatred grows: "So cool she looked now; so triumphant. He was full of hate for her." As she returns home Jane has a sudden recognition of her foolishness: "She thought: I've been playing with fire."

After Jane leaves, Ahmed turns to Bryant for sexual and psychological comfort. Naipaul describes Bryant as "very ugly, damaged from birth, who expressed all that [Ahmed] saw of himself in certain moods." Ahmed's compulsive writing begins to incorporate the recent events into his apocalyptic vision. One of the interesting personae that Ahmed contrives in his journal is that of a worshipful middle-class white woman seeking his blessing. In a dialogue with her he says, "*You think you will play with the little black boys and then you will go home, but I've news for you, Clarissa, the little black boys are not playing anymore.*" Like Malik, who suspected that Benson was a spy, Ahmed asks Clarissa if her father was in intelligence. His paranoia grows and festers in his writings and his sexual inadequacy is sublimated into a fantasy of social violence: "The whole place is going to blow up. I cannot see how I can control the revolution now. When everybody wants to fight there is nothing to fight for. Everybody wants to fight his own little war, everybody is a guerrilla." His murderous contempt for Clarissa (Jane) is seen in his description of her as "rotten meat," an image reminiscent of

Bobby's hatred and fear of female sexuality in *In a Free State*. Having relieved himself in his writing, Ahmed puts his face close to Bryant, who has grown jealous of Jane's attention to his lover, and in a chilling sentence that foreshadows the horrific conclusion of the novel, he says to the boy, "I'll give her to you."

The pace of the novel then slows considerably as Naipaul spends many pages examining the characters of Roche and Jane, how they came to meet, their romantic hopes and narrow sensibilities, and their growing dissatisfaction with their present lives. The reader is relieved when he finally sees and hears the characters move and speak for themselves once again. Naipaul much more effectively conveys their minds through his dramatic scenes, their quiet or angry conversations, than through his third-person analysis.

Roche begins to recognize the hollowness of his life and his failure as a liberal to reshape the racial attitudes of the world about him. "I've built my whole life on sand," he sadly reflects. Not only is he not a doer, he waits upon events to shape his life. Furthermore, knowing that Jane plans to return to England, he feels that he has failed to establish a significant relationship with a woman who once looked up to him. Now he finds himself trapped in a lost corner of the world and wants out.

Jane, however, has detached herself from Roche's failure. She had once attempted to convey her "hysterical vision of the world" to the seemingly secure residents of the island's Ridge, an exclusive section of the island that looks down upon the poverty and disorder of the town. Naipaul characterizes her ideas as impressionistic and passionate but without any pattern or conclusion. Having enjoyed another cycle of adventure and now bored and uneasy in her surroundings, she has become "calm, detached, the visitor." For the second time Naipaul compares her to the "sea anemone, rooted and secure, waving its strands at the bottom of the ocean," an image that prepares the reader for her fatal attraction of Jimmy Ahmed into her inadequate embrace.

Naipaul exhibits an intense disgust with Jane's arrogant sense of security and sexuality, reminiscent of his feelings toward Linda in *In a Free State*. At times she is pathetic and at others she is repulsive. Consider, for example, Naipaul's description of her in the following scene. Roche and Jane are visiting their only friend on the island, Harry de Tunja, when Roche leaves his hammock to retrieve his sunglasses from the house. When he enters the bedroom he finds Jane naked from the waist down:

> She glanced at Roche as he came in; then, turning her back to him, and facing the window, she seemed about to sit on the bed. She came down hard on the very edge of the bed, which dipped below her weight; but she didn't sit; she threw herself backward in an apparently abandoned attitude, opened her legs, raising her feet up against the wall, and inserted what Roche now realized was the tampon she held in her hand; and then almost immediately she was sitting, had seized the blue plastic tampon case from the bed and sent it spinning with a low, level flick of the wrist to the corner of the room where their basket was, with their beach things. The tampon case struck the concrete wall and clattered on the floor.[7]

The earlier sordid sexual encounter with Ahmed and her being characterized as "rotten meat" combine with this scene to prepare the reader for her final degradation at the hands of Ahmed and Bryant. One can only wonder at the degree to which Naipaul's own sense of rootlessness and insecurity contributed to the grotesque portraits of such women as Linda and Jane.

While Jane and Roche are visiting Harry, a man named Meredith stops by. A middle-aged black man, a solicitor who hosts a radio interview program, Meredith once worked for the BBC and recalls his interview with Jimmy Ahmed in London. He points out that Ahmed was manipulated by an upper-class white woman who turned him into her "little Pekingese black." "I really should have interviewed her," he says, "but I just recorded the yapping." Meredith's analysis of Ahmed derives from Naipaul's own commentary upon Malik. Ahmed is dangerous because he retains some of the English glamour and because "he's nothing at all." Prophetically, Meredith observes that "There's a kind of dynamic about his condition that has to work itself out. In England it ended with rape and indecent assault. The same dynamic will take him to the end here." Throughout the novel Naipaul nicely blends images of social chaos and violence with those of sexual disorder and violence. To that extent, Ahmed's character is of a piece.

Naipaul handles the subject of violence in this novel in a very interesting manner. He depicts the large-scale violence in the town through indirection. With chilling detachment, however, he presents a close-up and detailed account of Jane's rape and murder. After one of the young gang leaders named Stephens is killed by the police the tension that has been mounting in the town finally breaks loose. The usual wave of music from the radios ceases and "the reggae party was at last over. Far away, the airport, fading into haze, showed two white planes. Jane thought: I've left too late." And so the violence begins. Jane's return ticket to England, her sense of security, is useless now. She and Roche retreat to the Ridge where they stay in telephone contact with Harry in an attempt to piece together the violent story unfolding below in the town.

Harry informs them that no one knows what is happening or is going to happen. He does report, however, that after the police shot Stephens, Ahmed started walking around the town carrying the boy's body and gathering a large procession. In the evening Jane could see silent explosions of smoke and small fires growing in the city. Harry again reports by phone that the people have gone crazy and are burning shops. A few people, but no one knows who, have escaped by plane. There is no leadership among the violent groups for, as Harry explains, "Everybody down there is a leader now." There is no rational plan, no grand cause, only small violent groups expressing their hatred and frustrations. Ahmed himself has retreated to his Grange. Harry explains that "Jimmy was always washed up here. . . . I don't know what they told him in London. But at a time like this he is just another Chinaman." Eventually American helicopters begin flying in over the town. It is in the interests of the United States to maintain order on the island so as to protect its interests in the bauxite industry.

Naipaul manages to develop the sense of fear, confusion, and anxiety through this limited perspective on the violence below the Ridge. Harry's telephone calls and Roche's and Jane's distant view of the town from the Ridge are the major sources of information about what is happening. The main characters become enveloped in a world of fearful rumors. Reason and understanding are paralyzed and displaced by a growing sense of fatalism. In *In a Free State* Naipaul employed this same technique with perhaps even more effect. Bobby's and Linda's view of the deadly changes going on around them is more severely limited through their isolated drive through Africa but Naipaul's narrative technique has a similar effect.

After some degree of order is restored in the town, Roche meets Meredith to be interviewed on his radio program. This interview allows Naipaul to explore Roche's evaluation of himself after his experiences on the island. Roche's growing hatred of Jane no longer allows her to be a suitable confidante. In fact, one evening while they are watching the fires in the town he turns to her and says, "Yes, it's going up in flames. But it's taking you with it." Roche explains to Meredith that he feels like a stranger here, that he hoped there were racial problems here he could solve, work for him to do. He admits now, however, that the idea of agricultural reform cannot work, that the idea is antihistorical because all over the world people are leaving the land to go to the cities. Roche wishes his life had taken a different direction and now that it is too late he has come to realize that he has never really been in charge of his life, that he has been driven by circumstances, including those that made him into a hero among the South African resistance. Like so many of Graham Greene's heroes, Roche is driven by his fear of failure and now recognizes that his life has, indeed, been built upon sand. Meredith observes that Roche's book has a simple message: "You transgressed; you were punished; the world goes on." The pain and suffering that Roche endured, Meredith says, may have brought him a kind of personal peace but "it's a dead end. . . . It doesn't hold out hope for the rest of us."

When Meredith asks Roche if he has really come to terms with his past experiences, Roche responds with a remarkable and devastating honesty: "I haven't come to terms with it. All my life I've been frightened of pain. Of being in a position where pain could be inflicted on me." He finally ends the interview with the observation that he does not believe in guerrillas, that he quickly dismissed Ahmed's Grange as a cover for them, and that he simply "believed in the gangs." No sooner does he say this than he regrets it, for he knows that this remark will wound the boy Stephens's mother if she hears it on the radio. When he returns home he reflects on the illusion of security and stability in the world: "For all of them [Meredith, Jane, myself] the world was fragile. And there had been a calamity."

The next day Roche tells something to Jane that reveals his cowardice and that marks his presence in the island as that of a refugee from fear. Shortly after the publication of his book he is visited by a man who claims to be a reporter. It turns out that the man, a large, powerful figure, came to threaten Roche. He told him that he had better get out of England because he was going to be killed. And so, Roche came to the West Indian island primarily to save his life and not to solve its racial problems. Upon hearing this, Jane turns on him saying, "And now you'll just leave Jimmy out there for those people to kill," and announces that Ahmed has been her lover.

Naipaul next presents a final glimpse into Ahmed's devastated mind as he writes to Marjorie, the woman in England who "made me a man for the first time." "I am dying alone and unloved," he writes, "and I will die in anger, no other way is possible now." He explains his love for Bryant and how the boy has gone mad with grief over the death of his friend Stephens, a death he blames on Ahmed. He describes how he leaves Bryant's food outside of the door and how he comes like a dog to eat it, letting Ahmed know that he has a cutlass with which he will murder him. Ahmed is overwhelmed with the multiple betrayals he has experienced and focuses them at this point upon Marjorie: "You shouldn't have let me down Marjorie, you shouldn't have sided with the others. I didn't want to hate you like the others . . . you made me and then you made me feel like dirt again, good only for dirt."

While in this mood of despair, anger, and desolation Ahmed discovers Jane at his door. Planning a brief, final visit, she dismisses her taxi and her last link to safety. In a matter of minutes she and Ahmed are in bed together, only this time Ahmed forces anal intercourse upon her, a scene that Naipaul describes in grotesque detail. "You're a virgin, Jane," he shouts. "We're breaking you in today, Jane." She cries out in pain and Ahmed says softly, "You are rotten meat." After sodomizing her, Ahmed walks her to a derelict section of the Grange where there is a ramshackle latrine. The smell of urine and decay permeates the atmosphere. He is bringing her there as a peace offering to Bryant: "Bryant and I are not friends now, Jane. You'll help to make us friends." Sitting in the shadows is Bryant: "His face was twisted and he wore the pigtails of aggression. . . . He had a cutlass in his hand and he was in tears."

Ahmed locks his right arm around Jane's neck and calls out to Bryant to "Kill the rat . . . Your rat, Bryant! Your rat!" Bryant makes his first cut on her right arm: "Sharp steel met flesh. Skin parted, flesh showed below the skin, for an instant mottled white, and then all was blinding, disfiguring blood, and Bryant could only cut at what had already been cut." When Ahmed feels Jane's body go limp "a desolation began to grow on him. And then there was nothing but desolation." They dump her body in the dry pit of the septic tank and cover her over with dirt. A life of anger, frustration, sexual perversion, ambition, and self-delusion has come into focus in this insane act of sodomy and murder. Ahmed knows there is nowhere to go now, that it is only a matter of time before the police will come to get him.

In the meantime, however, Roche shows up at the Grange. Seeing that something is wrong but not quite understanding what, he thinks, "This place has become a slaughter-ground," and he heads back to his house seeking safety. He finds Jane's ticket and passport and tries to dispose of them. He calls Harry and lies, saying that Jane has left him, leaving her clothes behind but taking her ticket and passport. Harry reminds him that since Jane was eased past customs by some Americans, there is no official record of her being in the country. Roche's attempt to destroy her ticket and passport is a symbolic gesture to invalidate her arrogance, her sense of security, her English hiding place from the present reality. When Ahmed telephones him, however, he tells him not to try to come to his place, that the police will arrest him, and then foolishly adds: "I'm leaving you alone. That's the way it's going to be. We are leaving you alone. I am leaving. I am going away. Jane and I are leaving tomorrow. Jane is in her room packing. We are leaving you here. Are you hearing me? Jimmy?" Jimmy merely replies, "Massa," and the novel ends.

One assumes that Roche returns to England and eventually Ahmed and Bryant are arrested and Jane's body is discovered. Unlike the Malik case, however, the conclusion of the novel is left up in the air, with the final focus upon Roche as a confused, rootless man, a white counterpoint to the insane, programmed, half-breed Jimmy Ahmed. Both men are involved in Jane's death. Both men are failures. None of the characters or events in this novel offers hope. It is a dark, cynical piece of writing that suggests a fatalistic worldview. One of the games that Meredith plays with Harry, Jane, and Roche, is to ask them what they would do with one wish. He tells them that he will write down the answer to all of their wishes. After they elaborate on their desires, he reads his answer: "*The life being described is the life the speaker lives or a life he has already lived. The setting may change, but no one will make a fresh start or do anything new.*" Meredith expresses here an idea of determinism that has troubled Naipaul for years, an idea, as will be seen, that he returns to in his later novels.

Naipaul is very concerned with the subject of violence in fiction. In a 1964 essay he wrote:

> The violence some of us are resisting is not the violence which is a counter of story-telling. It is the violence which is clinical and documentary in intention and makes no statement beyond that of bodily pain and degradation. It is like the obscene photograph. It deals anonymously with anonymous flesh, quickened only by pleasure or pain; and this anonymity is a denial of art.[8]

In both *In a Free State* and *Guerrillas* Naipaul distances the broad social violence by focusing upon the limited perspective of his main characters. When he presents graphic scenes of violence, such as that of Bobby's beating at the hands of the African military or the sodomizing and murder of Jane, he does indeed attempt to place the scenes within a significant social and artistic context. He goes on to write that

> the artist who, for political or humanitarian reasons, seeks only to record abandons half his responsibility. He becomes a participant; he becomes anonymous. He does not impose a vision on the world. He accepts; he might even make romantic; but he invariably ends by assessing men at their own valuation. The time comes when he is content to communicate the egoism of the brute.[9]

From the very beginning of *Guerrillas* Naipaul makes it clear that Jane is playing with fire, that her arrogance and detachment are fragile commodities in this dangerous West Indian world. Her murder is a punishment for her foolishness, for her profound ignorance of a culture and people foreign to her shallow sensibilities, for her selfish and playful involvement with a sexual psychotic. Moreover, the sodomizing and murder of Jane are a logical extension of the deep madness of Jimmy Ahmed. She comes to embody all of the desires, fears, and hatreds that ruled his life. By degrading her, possessing her, and then giving her away to his homosexual lover, Ahmed recapitulates in microcosm the course of his entire life. As Meredith pointed out, one's wish is determined by his past.

Naipaul, nevertheless, created quite a stir among critics with *Guerrillas* and he attempts to rationalize the painful sexual and violent scenes as follows:

> The novel [*Guerrillas*], you know, hangs between two sexual scenes. The first explains the second. I was very nervous before I wrote the first one. And I was appalled by the second. I hope I was careful enough to remove from the sex scenes any association of the standard erotic writing. But I was appalled. Yet I couldn't remove all of the more erotic or excitatory associations of words. I know it's offended a lot of people. It really has. But you see, the terror of that book is inevitable. It's a book about lies and self deception and people inhabiting different worlds or cultures. It is the only book I know which is really about an act of murder. That is why it's shocking—and the fact that it shocks you is part of its success. But it's the wrong kind of success if you think, God she was such an unpleasant girl. If she was really all that unpleasant, if you hadn't been made to understand her, you wouldn't have found her death to be so appalling.[10]

While these observations are essentially on the mark, it is not at all clear that Naipaul has made Jane anything more than an unpleasant woman. He very begrudgingly presents scenes in which she displays a compassionate humanity or even simple innocence. She has a tender moment with Roche after he returns from his interview with Meredith: "She surprised him like this sometimes, when she appeared to be natural and easy, another person, obeying instincts that had suddenly risen within her. The occasions were rare and abrupt, and remained separate from the rest of their life together." That night she washes his hair: "no sex followed; they had been like children playing house." Such scenes are, indeed, rare, and Naipaul's overall image of Jane is one of a selfish romantic who uses men to entertain her, to carry her from one small adventure to another. Her character is understandable and almost comes to life, but compared to someone like Jimmy Ahmed, she remains artistically incomplete, a kind of white Englishwoman scapegoat for the frustrations and rage of an imagined mad, failed, black-power leader of the Third World.

To some extent *Guerrillas* is too conditioned by *In a Free State.* Linda and Bobby, Jane and Roche, a pair of outsiders, refugees, so to speak, are forced to come to grips with the developing menace of their exotic worlds. Bobby and Roche are both failures, half men who could not stick it out in England and who escaped to the Third World for the security and sense of superiority it afforded them. Linda and Jane are both unattractive Englishwomen whose adventures are always circumscribed by a sense of a safe harbor—in Linda's case the compound, in Jane's, the return ticket to England. What makes *Guerrillas* unique and gives it its driving force is the character of Jimmy Ahmed. By presenting him from three different perspectives—through his own writings, through his actions and dialogue, and through the eyes of the other characters—Naipaul brings his character to life. The reader understands, fears, and almost pities him in the final scenes. Perhaps that is what is so appalling about the murder of Jane. She becomes the inevitable victim of Ahmed's twisted passion, and the witnessing of her suffering reinforces one's understanding of Ahmed's mind and makes her death a necessary conclusion to this darkest of Naipaul's visions.

A Bend in the River

In January 1975 Naipaul visited Zaire and recorded his impressions of this new African nation (formerly the Belgian Congo) in an incisive essay entitled "A New King for the Congo: Mobutu and the Nihilism of Africa," published in the *New York Review of Books.* In Zaire Naipaul entered several worlds at once: the Congo of Joseph Conrad, a writer whose clear insights into that country and into human character fascinated Naipaul since childhood; the Africa of the bush, seemingly eternal and indomitable despite Arab and Belgian attempts to civilize it; and the new Africa, the so-called authentic Africa of Joseph Mobutu. Naipaul quickly penetrates the rhetoric and propaganda of the new government, the ostentatious facades of the new art and architecture of Zaire, and exposes Mobutu's kingship as a temporary reign of self-aggrandizement, greed, and terror. Naipaul's experiences in Zaire and his critical essay on Mobutu, combined with his personal obsessions with such themes as the mingling of different cultures, the deterioration of dreams, sexuality, and personal and social insecurity, went into the creation of his next novel, *A Bend in the River.* A brief account of "A New King for the Congo" may provide a few insights into the novel, especially the sense of fear and instability created in the fiction through the unseen character of the "Big Man," the figure drawn after Mobutu.

Naipaul opens his essay with a comment on the linguistic corruption of names in this new country, a corruption later paralleled by his descriptions of the government and its new culture. "Zaire," he explains, is a nonsense name, a sixteenth-century Portuguese corruption, according to Zarois, of a local word for "river." Furthermore, the Congo River is now called the Zaire as well, as is the local currency, which, Naipaul cynically reports, "is almost worthless."

Joseph Mobutu, whose father was a cook, worked himself up through the Congolese National Army to become a general, and, in 1965, he seized power. Abandoning the name of Joseph, he became known as Mobutu Sese Seko Kuku Ngbendu Wa Za Banga. The last five words in his new African name are a reference to his sexual virility, a necessity for an African chief. In public he always appears wearing a leopard-skin cap and carrying a symbolically carved stick, emblems of his African chieftaincy. As Naipaul describes him, "He rules; he is grand; and, like a medieval king, he is at once loved and feared. . . . Like Leopold II, Mobutu owns Zaire."

In the early 1970s Mobutu decided on a "radicalization of the revolution." During the initial revolution he had nationalized all businesses and plantations owned by foreigners—Greeks, Portuguese, and Indians—and had given them to the Zairois. A year later, Naipaul writes, "Mobutu, speaking the pure language of revolution, seemed to threaten everybody. . . . Against this new Zairois bourgeoisie—which he had himself created—the chief now declared war." The country is thus kept in a state of constant anxiety and fear, with many people with much to lose: "Stern men, these Zairois, nervous of the visitor, easily affronted, anxious only to make it known that they were loyal, and outdone by no one in their 'authenticity,' their authentic Africanness."

Throughout the essay Naipaul is always mindful of the indomitable African bush, the inscrutable and ancient world glimpsed by Conrad's Marlow and Naipaul's Linda. For all their talk of authenticity and the ways of ancestors, Naipaul observes, the Zairois feared "to be returned from the sweet corruptions of Kinshasa [the capital of Zaire] to the older corruption of the bush, to be returned to Africa. And the bush is close. It begins just outside the city and goes on forever." While on the river Naipaul observed the Congo hyacinth, a water plant that first appeared in the upper Congo in 1956 and has since spread all the way down, "treacherously, beautiful, with thick lilylike green leaves and a pale-lilac flower like a wilder hyacinth." As it chokes the river and clogs the propellers of the steamers, Naipaul views the hyacinth as a symbol of the encroaching bush: "If the steamers do not fail, if there are no more wars, it is the Congo hyacinth that may yet imprison the river people in the immemorial ways of the bush." Despite the attempts of the Europeans to civilize Africa and despite African nationalists following in the footsteps of European corruption, "Everyone feels the great bush at his back. And the bush remains the bush, with its own logical life." As will be seen, Naipaul incorporates this theme and the image of the water hyacinth into his novel. While Linda in *In a Free State* had a fearful glimpse of the immemorial bush from the car window, in *A Bend in the River* Naipaul allows his hero, Salim, to penetrate a bit more deeply into its encompassing presence. Even he, however, remains an outsider looking in.

As in the novel, Naipaul describes the flashy and absurdly modern buildings of the "presidential domain" of Nsele. Looking like a resort development the domain offers large meeting halls, swimming pools, lounges, and excessively grand office buildings. In the new palace for visiting heads of state the baths are gold-plated. In the presidential park at Mont Ngaliema (formerly Mount Stanley) Naipaul observes the guards in their decorative uniforms and the gates decorated with bronze plaques: "—the bad art of modern Africa: art that no longer serves a religious or magical purpose attempts an alien representationalism and becomes mannered and meaningless."

Everyone is in Zaire for money. Like the Europeans before him, the modern African seeks to surround himself with the emblems of wealth and power: the Mercedes, the expensive suit, fatter prostitutes, the gold-rimmed glasses, the large gold wristwatch, and "the big belly that in a land of puny men speaks of wealth." In the midst of this "unreal world of imitation" (p. 208) Naipaul observes a man named Simon, whose large company had been nationalized and who now works as its manager. (In the novel, Salim's shop is nationalized and because it is given to a man who is incapable of running it, Salim is hired to manage it.) Simon, who has a background of the bush, is educated, young, successful and possesses a new sense of himself and his African dignity but finds himself "adrift and nervous" in the artifice of Zaire. Naipaul sees Simon as symbolic of the potential new rage. Simon is vulnerable and dangerous because his resentment, which he cannot articulate, could "be converted into a wish to wipe out and undo, an African nihilism, the rage of the primitive men coming to themselves and finding that they have been fooled and affronted."

Mobutu, according to Naipaul, is "the great African nihilist," who seeks authenticity by refusing to borrow a conscience, a soul, or a language in his attempt to restore ancestral ways and "recreate that pure, logical world." But what Mobutu gives, he can and does take away, and his people worship him, fear him, and go along with his fantasy. Meanwhile, Mobutu extends his power, has his image mass-produced and posted everywhere, has new palaces and parks built to embody his dreams of future magical power. "Mobutuism honors only one man: the chief, the king." Mobutuism simplifies the world: it plunders the inherited Belgian state, confiscates and nationalizes property, and distributes jobs to friends and allies. "The kingship of Mobutu has become its own end," Naipaul concludes. "To arrive at this sense of a country trapped and static, eternally vulnerable, is to begin to have something of the African sense of the void. It is to begin to fall, in the African way, into a dream of a past—the vacancy of river and forest."

Many critics, including John Updike, think that *A Bend in the River* marks an advance over the much-praised *Guerrillas*. Updike finds it "broader, warmer, less jaded and kinky . . . though not quite as vivid and revelatory as the fiction in 'In a Free State.' "[11] Like *In a Free State, A Bend in the River* extends Naipaul's image of Africa as a dangerous continent that is winding down, a desperate world unable to rise from corruption and from the bush. In Updike's words, it is "an Africa of withering colonial vestiges, terrifyingly murky politics, defeated pretensions, omnivorous rot, and the implacable undermining of all that would sustain reason and safety."[12]

The hero of the novel, Salim, comes from a coastal Muslim family that in its customs was closer to the Hindus of northwest India, from which it originally came centuries ago. As a narrator, then, he is established as both an African and an outsider for, as he points out, the coast is not truly African but an area established by the Arabs, Indians, Persians, and Portuguese. "True Africa was at our back," in the interior. Nazruddin, a family friend, offers Salim his abandoned shop in the interior, at the bend in the river, in a settlement that has been half destroyed during the violence after independence. Salim travels to the interior, takes over the shop, and the novel describes his life there during the next seven years, during the peace, before violence and social chaos once again return.

He befriends some Indian families, trades with a mysterious character named Zabeth, a magician from downriver, and agrees to look after her son, Ferdinand, who attends school at the local lycée. He soon acquires a living companion when his family, which breaks up and dissipates during a social revolution on the coast, sends him their slave, Ali, who takes the new name of Metty (a name that means "someone of mixed race"). Salim later befriends a white couple, Raymond and Yvette. Raymond works for "Big Man" (the Mobutu figure) and is his closest white personal friend. He manages a university in the Domain, a group of new buildings in the town's former white suburb. Salim seduces Yvette and their affair develops into a passionate but unfulfilling relationship.

The failed relationship with Yvette and events that follow reduce Salim to a state of near despair and, in order to find relief and rescue from his disordered state of mind, he flies to London to visit his old friend Nazruddin, who is now involved in real estate there. Salim agrees to become engaged to marry Nazruddin's daughter (the original reason for Nazruddin's generosity in turning his shop in Africa over to Salim) but, more importantly, he is struck by the happiness of his friend who has settled so comfortably into the life of London. Salim now becomes even more convinced than ever that his own life will never be secure, at peace.

When he returns to Africa he discovers that government corruption, greed, and terror have once more swept the land and that his shop has been confiscated and turned over to a black "Citizen," who, in turn, hires Salim to manage the business. Salim's life becomes progressively more miserable as the foolish new owner begins to assert his power over him. Meanwhile, rumors begin to fly that a revolution is brewing, and everyone sets about making as much money as he can, however he can.

Salim himself becomes corrupt, and is caught by the police for smuggling ivory. Lacking enough money to pay the bribe, he is imprisoned. He is eventually released from prison by Ferdinand, who has risen to become one of the officials in Big Man's government. Reminiscent of the character of Simon in Naipaul's essay "A New King for the Congo," Ferdinand is educated, young, proud, but finds himself adrift and anxious, recognizing the deterioration around him, sensing the chaos that is threatening to undo all that he has studied and worked for. The novel ends with an impending revolution that may again bring massive killings and, perhaps, even the destruction of Big Man himself. Ferdinand, filled with disillusionment and rage, warns Salim to flee the country. Recognizing the danger and futility of remaining in Africa now, Salim boards a steamer and heads presumably toward London, a refugee from social and psychic disorder.

Salim opens his narrative with the statement: "The world is what it is; men who are nothing, who allow themselves to become nothing, have no place in it." Elaine Campbell makes a perceptive observation about the tone of the novel that is established here. Salim's opening credo reflects an interesting duality in his nature. Unlike Singh in *The Mimic Men,* Salim is only remotely Indian and possesses African loyalties that accrue from his family's long history on the coast. His acceptance of the world as it is reflects his Indian sense of resignation. On the other hand, his contempt for men who allow themselves to become nothing reflects his African admiration for the strong man. He can therefore be used by Naipaul, Campbell argues, to narrate without condemnation the actions of the Big Man. "In other words," she concludes, "he can be simultaneously involved and detached. It is Salim's detachment in spite of personal damage that provides Naipaul with the medium for control of tone."[13] Thus Naipaul can modulate through artistic distancing his more immediate and bitter feelings expressed in "A New King for the Congo."

Like Naipaul himself, Salim recalls that from an early age he acquired the habit of detaching himself from a familiar scene and considering it from a distance, a point of view that gives him an understanding of himself in relation to his society. "It was from this habit of looking," Salim says, "that the idea came to me that as a community we had fallen behind. And that was the beginning of my insecurity." Here again is one of Naipaul's most persistent themes, the fragility and insubstantiality of human life and of Third World society itself. Salim is well aware of the news of rebellions and explosions of rage taking place throughout other sections of Africa and concludes that "the political system we had known was coming to an end, and that what was going to replace it wasn't going to be pleasant. I feared the lies—black men assuming the lies of white men."

Salim is envious of his well-to-do friend Indar, who informs him that he is going away to England to study at a famous university (which recalls Naipaul's own escape from Trinidad). Indar tells Salim, "We're washed up here, you know. To be in Africa you have to be strong. We're not strong. We don't even have a flag." It is against such a backdrop of insecurity and fear that Salim decides to leave the coast and head into the interior: "I had to break away from our family compound and our community. To stay with my community, to pretend that I had simply to travel along with them, was to be taken with them to destruction. I could be master of my fate only if I stood alone . . . —another tide of history was coming to wash us away." Like Naipaul, Salim has the historical sense of cultural futility—the previous inroads of such foreign cultures as the Arabs and the Belgians were already washed away—and, as he later discovers, the lives of the people he left behind on the coast are shattered by another revolution. Again, like Naipaul, Salim seems to have no lasting home and at the conclusion of the novel he follows in the footsteps of his creator and flees to London, an island of security for the expatriate.

The sense of dislocation in the novel is strong and is painfully realized by Salim. Upon his arrival in the interior he becomes friends with an elderly Indian couple whose family had all left during the troubled period of independence. This couple seems suspended and isolated in a dreamworld: "The bush of Africa was outside their yard; but they spoke no French, no African language, and from the way they behaved you would have thought that the river just down the road was the Ganges, with temples and holy men and bathing steps." They seem oblivious to the ravages brought about by the move to independence. Salim, on the other hand, is unnerved by "the depth of that African rage, the wish to destroy, regardless of the consequences."

One of Salim's first customers is Zabeth, a woman from a fishing village in the bush, who travels sixty miles to his shop to purchase goods that she retails in her village. She is a mysterious, self-contained woman, a magician or sorceress, who comes to represent for Naipaul an emissary of "the true, safe world, protected from other men by forest and clogged-up waterways." Every man in the bush, he continues, "knew that he was watched from above by his ancestors, living forever in a higher sphere, their passage on earth not forgotten, but essentially preserved, part of the presence of the forest. In the deepest forest was the greatest security."

Unlike Zabeth, Salim's insecurity continues to grow throughout the novel, despite his attempts to find fulfillment in his affair with Yvette or comfort in his friend Indar's philosophy to live in the present and trample the past. Shortly after he arrives in the interior Salim learns from Metty that his family has dispersed because of a violent uprising in the area, the stability of centuries undermined in mere days. Salim is truly on his own, although in the back of his mind he recalls Nazruddin, the family friend who gave him this chance at developing a business, a man who is a survivor of social crises. During Salim's years in the interior we hear that Nazruddin moves from Africa to Canada and finally to London. He is a vague role model for Salim, who, after much suffering and disillusionment, visits Nazruddin in London later in the novel in order to regain a sense of direction and hope.

The water hyacinths that Naipaul observed in his essay "A New King for the Congo" appear frequently throughout the novel. They seem to have appeared on the river as if by spontaneous generation, "dark floating islands on the dark river." They grow faster than men can destroy them, clogging the waterways and fouling the propellers of the steamers. Like the bush, the hyacinths represent African mystery and power, at odds with European incursions and African revolutions. It is among the thick clusters of the hyacinths that the body of Father Huismans is discovered in a dugout. His body had been mutilated and his head cut off and spiked. This grotesque image probably arose from the waking fantasy that Naipaul experienced about the time that he was planning this novel. He saw himself as a corpse tossing lightly among the reeds at the bottom of a river, "a river like the one in the Pre-Raphaelite painting of the drowned Ophelia." The painting he refers to is by John Everett Millais. In it Ophelia is floating face up among a crowd of water hyacinths and other colorful water plants. The image of Father Huismans's spiked head suggests an ironic reversal of the spiked heads of the African natives that surround the house of Mr. Kurtz in Conrad's *The Heart of Darkness*, a work that often asserts itself in Naipaul's African novels.

Father Huismans is a teacher at the lycée, where Ferdinand has enrolled. Although the lycée is a remnant of the colonial period, Father Huismans possesses a genuine relish for Africa and its traditions. He has amassed a large collection of African masks but only those that served specific religious purposes and only originals. Salim observes that although Father Huismans knows a great deal about African religion he does not seem concerned with the state of the country. "I began to think of him as a pure man. His presence in our town comforted me." One of the most positive characters in the novel, Father Huismans becomes a victim of his own purity, his naivete, and limited dedication to a religious-academic goal. As Salim observes, "His idea of civilization was also like his vanity. It had made him read too much in that mingling of peoples by our river; and he paid for it." Ferdinand, for example, echoing the views of the new African, the destroyer of European vestiges, remarks on Father Huismans's collection of masks: "It is a thing of Europeans, a museum. Here it is going against the god of Africans."

For a period during his childhood Ferdinand had lived with his father, a trader, in the south, in one of the mining towns. For reasons that are not clear—perhaps his father had died—he returned to the interior, to his mother. Although he was accepted into her tribe, he is a stranger in a new land. Salim observes that the Africans, who called up the war and who suffered the most from it, could at least cope with the hardships. They had their villages and tribes, "things that were absolutely theirs. They could run away again to their secret worlds and become lost in those worlds, as they had done before."

Ferdinand, Salim continues, "was almost as much a stranger in the town as I was."

Schooled at the lycée and then at the Domain, Ferdinand develops a powerful sense of self-importance. Although limited in his perceptions and historical awareness, he becomes an idealist who has committed his life to a new Africa under the leadership of Big Man and his flag of "authenticity." Salim watches him grow into this new role. At the Domain "an African . . . was a new man whom everybody was busy making, a man about to inherit." And so, for a while, Salim's identification with Ferdinand as a fellow stranger weakens. At the end of the novel, however, Naipaul brings the two characters together again as Ferdinand releases Salim from prison, tells him to flee the country, and expresses his profound disillusionment with the new government and his rage at having devoted his life to a fraudulent ideal. He says to Salim,

> We're all going to hell, and every man knows this in his bones. . . . I felt I had been used. I felt I had given myself an education for nothing. I felt I had been fooled. Everything that was given to me was given to me to destroy me. . . . But there is no place to go to.[14]

In this confession Naipaul again draws the kinship between Ferdinand and Salim: two men without a secure home or homeland, a place to go, two men derided by the foolishness and vanity of their own dreams and ideals.

Throughout the novel Salim is surrounded by violence or the threat of violence. He knows what Ferdinand comes to learn—that what the Big Man gives he can take away. In the eyes of many Africans he sees frustration, anger, and fear. Their rebellions raise a ruthless spectacle that he can never forget or ignore: "The rage of the rebels was like a rage against metal, machinery, wires, everything that was not of the forest and Africa. . . . It was the rage that made an impression—the rage of men tearing at metal with their hands."

It is against this backdrop of rage that Naipaul depicts the New Domain, the brave new world opened by Big Man. The ancient tribes are displaced by the new army, who see themselves "both as the new men of Africa and the men of the new Africa." The flag and the omnipresent portrait of the president are their new fetishes and source of authority. "They believed that, by being what they were, they had earned the right to take" and became ivory poachers and gold thieves. Despite the new forms of corruption, business in the interior begins to boom. Salim's friend, Mahesh, obtains the Bigburger franchise in the town and prospers. Salim's own shop flourishes. Before long he sees many of the new Africans wearing gold-rimmed glasses, gold watches, and gold rings. The lust for gold is in the air and is contagious.

Salim's life takes a new turn, however, when his childhood friend, Indar, pays him a visit. Educated and now living in England, Indar has come as a guest of the government to lecture at the Domain for one term. It is Indar who introduces Salim to Yvette and Raymond, a meeting that would affect the course of his life. Indar's philosophy is summarized in his recurrent observation about the past as a psychological death trap:

> you must stop grieving for the past. You see that the past is something in your mind alone, that it doesn't exist in real life. You trample on the past, you crush it. In the beginning it is like trampling on a garden. In the end you are just walking on ground. That is the way we have to learn to live now. (p. 113)

Indar's philosophy derives from the personal grief he experienced over his family's losses. During the coastal riots two generations of labor and achievement went to waste. The house built by his grandfather was taken; the risks and bravery of his father in creating a successful business out of nothing were rendered meaningless.

Indar concludes that his previous dream of home and security was "nothing more than a dream of isolation, anachronistic and stupid and very feeble." Feeling that he belongs to himself alone, he also chooses not to surrender his manhood to anybody: "We solace ourselves with that idea of the great men of our tribe, the Gandhi and the Nehru, and we castrate ourselves." Born to instability, suffering, and dreaming, Indar reasons that "for someone like me there was only one civilization and one place—London, or a place like it."

Indar's philosophy introduces an interesting dialectic into the novel, for it raises issues about Salim's own strong connections with the past. His servant-companion Metty is a constant reminder of Salim's past life on the coast. Salim's obsession with the mystery and security of tribal life in the bush also reflects his dream of a peaceful world whose customs and rituals are barriers to the present. (Salim, however, is keenly aware of his isolation from such an existence). It is also possible that through the interaction of Indar and Salim that Naipaul is still working out or at least dramatizing his ambiguous feelings toward his own past in the Caribbean. As Indar observes, planes are the allies of those who would trample upon the past and move quickly into new worlds, new lives, a dazzling transition that Naipaul experienced in his initial flight from Port of Spain to New York.

Naipaul's implicit evaluation of Indar's philosophy comes toward the end of the novel when Salim goes to London. He discovers from Kareisha, Nazruddin's daughter, that Indar's company has folded, putting him into a state of profound depression. On the coast as a boy his rich family made him feel "holy," she explains, and later the firm he worked for in England gave him that same sense. Now he feels lost and resentful. "From time to time that is all he knows," she explains to Salim, "that it is time for him to go home. There is some dream village in his head. In between he does the lowest kind of job." And so Indar fails to live according to his own philosophy, to trample the past. The past now consumes him.

Salim then adopts Indar's philosophy and modifies it to suit his own temperament: "That idea of going home, of leaving, the idea of the other place. . . . It was a deception. I saw now that it comforted only to weaken and destroy." He concludes that there is nothing to go back to: "We had become what the world outside had made us; we had to live in the world as it existed," an observation that echoes the opening sentence of the book. Naipaul's recurrent vision of a past becoming undone, of dreams unfolding a painful reality, serves to challenge the minds and hearts of many of his characters in other novels and becomes the chief focus of his next work, *The Enigma of Arrival,* where he comes to grips with that vision with a thoroughness and understanding only suggested in the earlier novels.

Unlike the more cynical Naipaul, Salim cannot help but find the Domain an exciting place. The people there seem to have their own way of seeing things and talking about them: "They were in touch with the world. To be with them was to have a sense of adventure." Having been isolated from a more sophisticated people, Salim begins to feel some of the romance and glory among this new crowd of people. Indar introduces him to Raymond, "the Big Man's white man," a historian who chronicles the sayings and doings of the president. His wife, Yvette, is in her late twenties, about Salim's age and half the age of her husband. Raymond is a shadowy, undeveloped character, whose scholarly dedication to history and to Big Man in particular, is finally undermined when Big Man no longer finds him politically useful. He is one of the many victims of Big Man's exploitative style, his ability to give and to take away.

At the time Salim meets Yvette his only sexual experiences have been those purchased at brothels. His first encounter with Yvette, however, opens up a new vision of sexuality and romance he has never known before. Yvette entertains Indar and Salim and her seductive presence, heightened by a Joan Baez recording, overwhelms Salim: "Even before the songs ended I felt I had found the kind of life I wanted; I never wanted to be ordinary again." Later, after Indar returns to London and Ferdinand goes off to the capital to take up his administrative cadetship, Salim and Yvette meet again and begin to enjoy a sexual relationship. At last, it seems, Salim has found a meaningful experience through which to reorder his life: "The sexual act became for me an extraordinary novelty, a new kind of fulfillment, continuously new. . . . I was full of the wonder of what had befallen me. . . . It was like discovering a great, unappeasable hunger in myself."

As in so many of Naipaul's novels, romance and sexuality quickly fail and lead to bitter disillusionment and anger. As insurrections crop up Raymond sees that he is a defeated man. The glorious Domain becomes a "house of death" and Yvette becomes restless, different. Naipaul describes the final scene between Yvette and Salim against this background of increasing anxiety in the town and government. Yvette pays an abrupt visit to Salim's place and her manner seems hurried and mechanical. "Affection, just before betrayal," Salim thinks. He explodes in a rage and violently beats her. She collapses on the bed weeping. Salim sits on the bed next to her, attracted and revolted by her at once:

> Her body had a softness, a pliability, and a great warmth. Only once or twice before had I known her like that. At this moment! I held her legs apart. She raised them slightly—smooth concavities of flesh on either side of the inner ridge—and then I spat on her between her legs until I had no more spit. (*BR*, p. 220)

Like Jimmy Ahmed, who spit into Jane's mouth, Salim expresses his contempt at the false promise of sexuality, its powerful force to cloud the mind while satisfying the body. Once again, Naipaul depicts the white European woman as a femme fatale. She offers hope, excitement, adventure, but she is uncommitted, foreign, exotic; and her betrayal of Third World men demands rage and contempt. Salim, of course, is hardly an innocent in all of this. He actively seduced her at the beginning and allowed his unhappiness to lead him deeper into the false dream of romance and sexual fulfillment. Much of his contempt and anger is unwittingly directed at himself.

Salim's world becomes more and more absurd after he loses Yvette. His friend Mahest and his wife, obsessed with their bodies (she became a recluse after acid blemished her face), have become cut off from the world. Their high Indian traditions no longer support them and now "they were empty in Africa, and unprotected, with nothing to fall back on. They had begun to rot." Salim recognizes that he is like them and that unless he acts right away he will share their fate. Images of decay permeate the novel and suggest that the larger social deterioration is mirrored in microcosm in the souls of men. Later, when Salim is arrested for smuggling ivory, the policeman who arrests him and demands a bribe explains that the "revolution had become *un pé pourrie*. A little rotten."

In order to escape this environment of disorder and decay Salim flies to London to talk to Nazruddin and to become engaged to his daughter. If Nazruddin's continued success and survival depress Salim, his discovery of Indar's failure strengthens him in his belief that one must accept the world as it is, that he must abandon the false dreams of security, a place to go, a renovating romance. "The younger Indar was wiser," he thinks. Later, when Ferdinand releases him from prison and confesses his own disillusionment, Salim finds that his philosophy is confirmed. The best he can hope for is to follow in the stoical but optimistic path of Nazruddin, to return to England, to start again in a world where there is a stable culture, a new interior to explore and learn to accept.

6

A Safe House in the Wood

Like his father and himself, many of the heroes of Naipaul's novels are writers. Obsessed since childhood with the idea of becoming a writer, Naipaul at first saw his vocation as one that would liberate him from the cultural poverty of Trinidad and allow him to enter the world of high culture in England. During the early years of his career, in the 1950s, he was a divided person: Naipaul the young man, filled with anxieties, ambitions, private fears and dreams, and Naipaul the writer, seeking to capture the sophisticated drama of life in his new world. While a youth in Trinidad he had developed fantasies about the role of the writer, and these were nourished during his first five years in England. As he writes, "The separation of man from writer which had begun on the long airplane flight from Trinidad to New York became complete." It was not until he began to write *Miguel Street* that he sensed man and writer coming together. Writing twenty eight years after the publication of *Miguel Street*, Naipaul makes this seemingly trite, but personally profound, observation: "Man and writer were the same person. But that is a writer's greatest discovery. It took time—and how much writing!—to arrive at that synthesis." Naipaul's great discovery is poignantly recorded in his autobiographical novel *The Enigma of Arrival*, a book that resolves and synthesizes many of the complex themes he was working out in the novels written during the previous thirty years.

Although he takes care to separate them from himself, the heroes of many of Naipaul's novels are writers, creators: Pundit Ganesh, Mr. Stone, Mr. Biswas, Ralph Singh, and Jimmy Ahmed. All of these characters embody aspects of Naipaul's obsession with his vocation as a writer, a vocation that is a sacred inheritance from his father that promises to bring him peace and fulfillment. Writing before the publication of *Guerrillas,* Paul Theroux makes this perceptive comment about Naipaul's self-reflexive characters:

> Creation, in Naipaul's terms, involves perception. The ability to assess oneself in one's setting is necessary if a person is to write well or make anything new; detail must be seen, judgments questioned. With these perceptions, the experience of something sighted, arrives a specific calmness which is resolution. In this calmness is the confident detachment which can result in creation: this still moment, which the creator occupies, makes it possible for the experience to be written about, or painted, or sculptured, given its true shape. For Ganesh, for Mr. Stone, Mr. Biswas and Singh, the ability to create comes slowly, but when it comes the moment is known, and the act of writing completes them, makes them whole; it exhausts and satisfies them.[1]

Theroux's observation, however, does not apply to *Guerrillas.* Jimmy Ahmed's rambling prose, filled with fantasies of sexual power, is masturbatory in nature. It provides him temporary relief to his manic moods, but in the end fails him, leaving him unfulfilled and fragmented. He then turns to rape and murder in a desperate attempt to enact his fantasies.

Despite his madness and despite the failure of his writing to complete and make him whole, Jimmy Ahmed also represents a facet of Naipaul's complex personality. In *The Enigma of Arrival* Naipaul writes: "The dream of exhaustion once; now the debilitation brought on by involuntary thoughts of the final emptiness. . . . It was as though the calling, the writer's vocation, was one that could never offer me anything but momentary fulfillment." Theroux's concept of the writer is much more romantic, definitive, and sentimental than that of Naipaul. As will be seen, Naipaul's sense of peace and fulfillment is defined within a landscape of constant change, a personal landscape shaped by the artist's mind. His childlike dream of a safe house in the woods is eroded by the melancholy perception of the evanescence of all things, including dreams and the seeming fulfillment of fiction.

Most of the reviewers of *The Enigma of Arrival* comment upon Naipaul's blurring the distinction between autobiography and fiction. One writer observes that in this book "Naipaul assumes the autobiographical role of social observer of mores and manners in a small village in these tales of ordinary lives and emotions." This writer goes on to say that the book is "less a novel than a rumination," a work that "breaks down the barriers between life and art."[2] Along similar lines, another reviewer writes that the book is "discursive and ruminative, more like an extended essay than a novel" and that "the intricately structured chapters in this highly autobiographical book reveal 'the writer defined by his . . . ways of seeing.' "[3]

Paul Gray goes a step beyond the previous reviewers and states that "although it is called a novel, *The Enigma of Arrival* stretches the line between fiction and autobiography nearly to the vanishing point. The unnamed narrator is a writer in his mid 50s, an Indian and a Hindu, born in Trinidad, educated at Oxford, who has traveled extensively and lived most of his adult life in England. This person, in other words, is indistinguishable from V. S. Naipaul."[4] Christopher Lehmann-Haupt, on the other hand, tries to find a rationale for the designation of the work as a novel: "I suppose one reason why Mr. Naipaul calls 'The Enigma of Arrival' fiction instead of autobiography is that its characters have probably been distorted from reality, if not wholly invented in some cases. But a more important purpose would be to emphasize the story's heightened effects instead of its more literal truth, even though contemporary nonfiction is increasingly availing itself of fictional techniques."[5]

Keeping closer to Naipaul's own rationale within the book, reviewer Jay Tolson observes, "If the modernist notion that the self is a fiction has become a cliché, it is to Naipaul's credit that he has given it new life. His labyrinthine narrative works through subtle indirection to show how he came to discover that a novelist's subject is ultimately himself—a truth lethal to a novelist who takes it too literally, but just as lethal if he never learns it."[6]

Shortly after he finished writing *The Enigma of Arrival* Naipaul published an essay in which he sets forth the aim of his novel:

> How, then, could I write honestly or fairly if the very words I used, with private meanings for me, were yet for the reader outside shot through with the associations of the older literature? I felt that truly to render what I saw, I had to define myself as a writer or narrator; I had to reinterpret things. I have tried to do this in different ways throughout my career. And after two

years' work, I have just finished a book in which, at last, as I think, I have managed to integrate this business of reinterpreting with my narrative. My aim was truth, truth to a particular experience, containing a definition of the writing self.[7]

In order to elucidate further what he is about in *The Enigma of Arrival,* Naipaul quotes from Marcel Proust's *Against Sainte-Beuve.* Proust's book is an attack upon Sainte-Beuve's critical approach, which argues that the personal details of a writer's life shed light upon his writings. Proust distinguishes between two selves: "a book is the product of a different self from the self we manifest in our habits, in our social life, in our vices." Sainte-Beuve's critical methodology, he argues, would impose trivial, superficial, and irrelevant details upon the more profound self embodied within the fiction:

It is the secretion of one's innermost life, written in solitude and for oneself alone, that one gives to the public. What one bestows on private life—in conversation, however refined it may be . . .—is the product of a quite superficial self, not of the innermost self which one can only recover by putting aside the world and the self that frequents the world.[8]

In their attempts to assimilate *The Enigma of Arrival* into their own experiences, the critics have overlooked the great significance that Proust holds for this work. In *Against Sainte-Beuve* Naipaul finds his abstract rationale for his novel. More important, however, is Proust's monumental cyclic novel *Remembrance of Things Past.* This work clearly served as the model for Naipaul's novel. Like *Remembrance of Things Past, The Enigma of Arrival* is an autobiographical interior monologue that traces the hero's development as a writer. It shares with its model philosophical, psychological, and sociological ruminations. More important, however, it shares a common theme that unifies both works: the vital connection between external and internal reality that is provided by time and memory. Like Proust, Naipaul is obsessed with the corrosive power of time to erode present reality and dreams, intelligence and ambitions. Memory preserves the past but fills one with anguish over the sense of loss. Furthermore, like Proust, he recognizes that memory distorts past experiences even while it synthesizes them. Both authors share the perception that one's desires ironically are the source of one's suffering and despair and that the isolated individual, faced with a false society extending false values, has art as his only refuge. Like Proust, Naipaul has implicitly raised the vocation of the novelist to that of a high priest practicing a religion that offers him—and his artistically rendered experiences and memories—both a dignity and an immortality.

Since the theme of *The Enigma of Arrival* is the author's attempt to come to grips with the idea of decay and death, it is appropriate that the novel spans a considerable period of time. The central focus of the book is upon the ten years that Naipaul lived in a cottage on the grounds of a Victorian-Edwardian manor in the Wiltshire valley, a short distance from Stonehenge and Salisbury Plain. After he completed his exhaustive study of Trinidad, *The Loss of El Dorado,* Naipaul had sold his house in England and set out to travel in the West Indies only to discover that his publisher wanted a book of another sort. Profoundly depressed over this disappointment, Naipaul wandered about for some months and finally settled into the quiet Wiltshire valley where, as a recluse, he hoped to regain some degree of self assurance and healing. During his ten-year stay in the cottage he observes the comings and goings of the various people connected with the manor, the natural beauty of the landscape, the passing of the seasons, and, most importantly, his own changing responses to the changing people and events surrounding him. In the process of this decade-long diary of his mind, he discovers the first real peace and sense of belonging he has ever enjoyed. No sooner does he reinterpret the world and find comfort in it than he begins to sense the drift of decay, a melancholy motion that carries away his second childhood, discovered in England, toward ruin and desolation.

The Enigma of Arrival is Naipaul's most mellow and philosophical novel. The sharp edge of irony and bitter cynicism of some of his early writings have been displaced here by a pervasive melancholy and musing upon human vanity induced by Naipaul's awakening to the reality of death. For more than thirty years, Naipaul says, since the death of his father in 1953, he lived without grief. Then he received the news that his younger sister in Trinidad had a brain hemorrhage and would not recover. It was her death that served as a catalyst for his novel:

My theme, the narrative to carry it, my characters—for some years I felt they were sitting on my shoulder, waiting to declare themselves and to possess me. But it was only out of this new awareness of death that I began at last to write. Death was the motif; it had perhaps been the motif all along. Death and the way of handling it—that was the motif of the story of Jack.[9]

The novel is divided into five sections. The first, "Jack's Garden," is a meditation upon a simple man named Jack, who lives in one of the cottages on the manor and who seems to define himself, in Naipaul's mind, in terms of his garden, where he was content to live out his life in celebration of the seasons. This section of the book also introduces some of the other main characters, such as Naipaul's elusive landlord, Mr. and Mrs. Phillips, the couple who looked after the manor, Pitton, the gardener, and Brenda and Les, a couple who did odd jobs around the manor. The next section, "The Journey," is Naipaul's account of his physical and metaphorical travel from Trinidad to England in order to become a writer. The third section, "Ivy," focuses upon Naipaul's reclusive landlord and the author's identification with him. It also presents a sympathetic study of Pitton, the gardener, and his enemy, Bray, the car-hire man. Alan, a literary man from London, also appears here. It is in this section that Naipaul reflects upon the many changes that have befallen the manor since his arrival, including the departure of Pitton and many alterations in the buildings and landscape. The fourth section, "Rooks," tells of Alan's suicide, Bray's acquisition of religion, the death of Mr. Phillips, the further deterioration of the manor, and the illness of the narrator. The last section, "The Ceremony of Farewell," is a very brief account of Naipaul's return to Trinidad after the death of his sister and his reflections upon mortality that eventually sponsored his writing the novel.

A reader's first pass through this novel may seem uneventful. There is no conventional plot to carry one along, no melodrama, and no commanding action. The story is unified through the developing perceptions of the narrator (whom I shall call Naipaul), his meditations upon details of character and landscape, his attempt to understand his present world in the light of his past and his past in light of the present, and his growing awareness that death is the mother of beauty. Naipaul observes that when he was a young man he was so eagerly seeking significant material to write about that he overlooked the great subjects all around him. He later discovers the important lesson that "great subjects are illuminated best by small dramas." That observation reveals the essence of Naipaul's technique in *The Enigma of Arrival.*

Naipaul moves into his cottage on the manor in the Wiltshire valley in 1970 and lives there for ten years. Like Thoreau, who abandoned his life in the metropolis "to front only the essential facts of life" at Walden, Naipaul retreats to a strangely bucolic countryside in order to take measure of his mind. (Interestingly, the name of the village and the manor on whose grounds Naipaul lives is Waldenshaw.) In both a literal and a metaphorical sense, however, Naipaul has to travel a much greater distance than did Thoreau to reach his safe house in the woods, and, once there, he remains in his pastoral chrysalis for nearly a decade before emerging from his "second childhood of seeing and learning." Although he has lived in England for twenty years, Naipaul is always aware of the fact that he comes from another hemisphere, that he is an alien, a man without a country. His life in Trinidad is now comprised of memories of a lost childhood to which he cannot, of course, ever return. England, the land of his youthful dreams of high culture, becomes the place where he realizes his ambitions as a writer but it is not his home. Here, in a cottage outside of Salisbury, he finally discovers a spot of time in which he experiences peace and fulfillment:

> The beauty of the place, the great love I had grown to feel for it, greater than for any other place I had known, had kept me there too long. . . . For me, for the writer's gift and freedom, the labor and disappointments of the writing life, and the being away from my home; for that loss, for having no place of my own, this gift of the second life in Wiltshire, the second, happier childhood as it were, the second arrival (but with an adult's perception) at a knowledge of natural things, together with the fulfillment of the child's dream of the safe house in the wood. (p. 88)

The novel opens with Naipaul's careful attention to the disparity between language and experience. Upon first arriving at the manor in winter he acknowledges that his perceptions of his surroundings are conditioned by his Caribbean childhood and by his knowledge of English literature and art. Those influences provided the forms of his perceptions, and, while they would continue to do so, he begins the slow process of reinterpreting his world in the light of new discoveries, new experiences that require new words, phrases, and learned associations. The river that runs past the property is called the Avon but "not the one connected with Shakespeare." "Later—when the land had more meaning," he goes on, "when it had absorbed more of my life than the tropical street where I had grown up—I was able to think of the flat wet fields with the ditches as 'water meadows' or 'wet meadows,' and the low smooth hills in the background, beyond the river, as 'downs.' " Throughout the novel Naipaul describes his new world in minute detail, noting the smallest flower or elusive animal. He does this not merely to create an atmosphere or to set a mood, but rather to establish himself as a child-adult narrator discovering the world and learning the language that expresses that world. "In my welcoming cottage," he says, "I was like a child again. As though I had at last, after twenty years, traveled to the equivalent of the fantasy I had had in mind when I left home."

When Naipaul meets Pitton, the gardener, and later learns that there were once sixteen gardeners on the manor, he is struck by the fact that Pitton does not look like a gardener. Upon further analysis, Naipaul realizes that his image of a gardener is based upon his memories of life in Trinidad. As a child he had seen few gardeners because in the Indian community where he lived there were no gardens. Sugarcane abounded everywhere. He did glimpse some gardens in Port of Spain but the men who worked in those gardens were essentially weeders and waterers, mostly Indians working barefoot. On the same level as "yard boys," they lacked dignity and distinction. And so, Pitton the gardener had to be reinterpreted and seen in a new light, even as the flat fields had to become "water meadows" and the smooth hills the "downs."

One of the main figures of the book is Jack, who lives with his wife in a farm worker's cottage. Naipaul is fascinated with Jack's contentment, his harmony with the seasons as he works his small garden, and his blindness to the decay and ruin surrounding him: "he had created a special land for himself, a garden, where (though surrounded by ruins, reminders of vanished lives) he was more than content to live out his life and where, as in a version of a book of hours, he celebrated the seasons." Naipaul sets against this image of a happy man his own melancholy perception: "although the life of the valley was just beginning for me, . . . I was also in a way at the end of the thing I had come upon. . . . I had grown to live with the idea that things changed; already I lived with the idea of decay."

A man in tune with the seasons and his landscape, Jack has found fulfillment, and Naipaul now becomes his understudy in a quest to do battle with time itself. What first seemed like an unchanging world, the life on the manor soon reveals that change is constant. People die, grow old, change houses, and Naipaul's own presence on the manor, he suddenly realizes, also introduces an element of change into its life. He then learns that Jack has become ill and over the weeks he sees his vegetable plot overrun with weeds, his fruit and flower garden grown wild. And so, the image of decay runs into the image of the contented man in harmony with the seasons. Knowing he is about to die, Jack declares that he wants to be with his friends for the last time and, with great effort, he dresses and drives to the local pub. Naipaul writes, "That final trip to the pub served no purpose except that of life; yet he made it appear an act of heroism; poetical."

Jack's death reinforces the narrator's sense of decay in all things, and he attempts to overcome his distress by focusing upon the constancy of change rather than upon decay—a rather abstract consolation. He acknowledges that it is his temperament that makes him see the certainty of ruin even at the moment of creation. He traces this sense of human vanity to the broken-down houses he lived in in Trinidad, the many moves his family made, and to his Indian heritage that asserts the world is outside of man's control. His fear of change conjures up his ancestral god: "the drum of creation in god's right hand, the flame of destruction in his left."

After presenting the images of the manor's dereliction and the death of Jack, Naipaul weaves another strand of mortality into his modern Ecclesiastes. Les and Brenda, a married couple who perform odd jobs around the manor, introduce the only element of melodrama in the novel though, in keeping with the tone of the book, Naipaul presents the subject in his usual understated way. From his limited perspective he reveals bits of information he gathers about Brenda and adds to those his own impressions of her, based upon casual encounters on the property. Brenda gives him the impression "of being at the center of passion, the cause of pain." She is an attractive young woman who is obsessed with her sexuality. She makes the narrator nervous and shows no regard for him (unlike the caretakers, the Phillipses, who see him as "artistic"). One day Mrs. Phillips informs Naipaul that Brenda has run off to Italy with another man. After some time passes, Mrs. Phillips discloses that Brenda's lover kicked her out, that she has returned to Les. Naipaul sees the couple together on several occasions and assumes all is well again. Later Mrs. Phillips gives him the news that Brenda is dead. Les has murdered her in the small cottage on the grounds. Naipaul's preoccupation with the idea of change, decay, and death is thus reinforced, even in this seemingly peaceful valley, within walking distance of the antiquity of Stonehenge and within sight and sound of a modern air force base.

Cutting in and out of the narrative are reflections on past characters and events, like refrains in a poem, to carry the meditative tone of the work forward. Thus, after recounting the murder of Brenda, the narrator returns to his thoughts of Jack: "Perhaps Jack's vision of the valley as a whole place would continue; a vision without the decadence that was in my eye; a vision of childhood that would expand in the adult mind." Nevertheless, he is keenly aware that his own time in the valley will come to an end, that his "second childhood of seeing and learning" will quickly be displaced within a middle-aged man coping with his own mortality. He allows these feelings to be represented in his response to the final destruction of Jack's house and garden, which have been leveled and poured with concrete as a forecourt to the big house: "So at last, just as the house was cleansed of Jack's life and death, so the ground he had tended finally disappeared."

Jack's life and death have revealed to Naipaul a significant aspect of creativity and change. Jack, he observes, "had created his own life, his own world, almost his own continent. But the world about him, which he so enjoyed and used, was too precious not to be used by others." He learns that the hold on the land that Jack and earlier people had is remarkably tenuous, and that each person creates his own ideal landscape, leaving it to be recreated in new forms by those people who follow.

Naipaul opens the next section of his novel, "The Journey," with a reflection upon Giorgio de Chirico's painting, entitled *The*

Enigma of Arrival, that serves as the structural basis for the entire book. The painting, which is reproduced on the jacket of the novel, depicts what appears to be a classical Mediterranean scene. In the background, beyond walls and gateways, one can see the top of a mast of an antique ship, presumably at a wharf. In the foreground there are two figures on a deserted street. Naipaul imagines that one of these muffled persons has just arrived and that the other is a native of the port, and he finds the scene to be one of mystery and desolation.

Naipaul thinks that one day he will write a story about the scene in that painting, and outlines it as follows: like the figure in the street, his narrator arrives at that classical port and moves from that desolation and silence through a gate. Upon entering the gate he is consumed by the sounds and life of a crowded city. His mission, perhaps family business or study, leads him into a series of adventures. Gradually he comes to realize that he has lost his purpose, that he is lost, and he begins to panic. Wanting to escape, he tries to get back to the ship but does not know how. At the moment of crisis he opens a door and finds himself back on the quayside where he first arrived. Finding the world as he remembered it and feeling himself saved, he suddenly realizes that one thing is missing: there is no mast, no sail above the walls. The ship has gone and the traveler has lived out his life.

This little parable sets forth the narrative structure of the novel, reflecting Naipaul's mental journey from Trinidad to London to Wiltshire, a journey that brings him face to face with the reality of his own mortality. Although his theme here is similar to that of Emily Dickinson's "Because I Could Not Stop for Death" and Dylan Thomas's "Fern Hill," Naipaul's paradoxical journey through time is more disturbing, self-conscious, dislocated, and panic-ridden.

Superficially, "The Journey" tells a story of Naipaul's travel from Trinidad to London, where he hoped to become a writer. More significantly, however, it chronicles his attempt to find fulfillment as a writer and a man, to find a way of having the writer consume the man, and to transform his anxieties, fears, and mortality into literary forms. Prior to describing his trip from Trinidad and his settling into London, Naipaul reflects upon the image of death that haunted him shortly before he began writing his novel. The idea of death came to him in his sleep, when he felt most vulnerable, and threatened to nullify all of his hopes and plans. His recent publication of the successful *In a Free State* not only did not alleviate these fears but seemed to increase them, leading him to conclude that "the calling, the writer's vocation, was one that could never offer me anything but momentary fulfillment."

The journey by ship from New York to Southampton focuses upon Naipaul's first piece of writing "based upon cosmopolitan material." Entitled "Gala Night," the essay describes a dance held on the last day at sea. Naipaul uses this essay to illustrate the point that as a young man, eager to capture great subjects and themes, he was unwittingly shutting himself off from the real, felt experiences out of which good literature arises. Thus he edits out of his memory the taxi driver who overcharged him in New York, the fear of aggressive or sexually unbalanced people who might have to share his cabin, the fear of being assaulted. Writer and man had not come together at this point.

His early days in London are joyless and lonely. Even as Constable had given him his idea of Salisbury, so now he knows London through Dickens's novels and illustrators. Art gives one the illusion of knowing a place, but the artist's vision is a distortion, a fantasy out of which everyone could construct his own world. Living in a boardinghouse, discovering that London is a strange and unknown place after all, and having lost the gift of fantasy, the dream of a future ideal world (he was *in* it), Naipaul turns his attentions toward a waitress, an Italian girl named Angela, who has a room in the boardinghouse. With the wisdom of hindsight, he berates himself for having devoted so much of his early writing to Angela's sexuality. What he allows to pass unrecorded during those days is the great movement of peoples that was beginning to take place, a movement between all the continents. Living at the boardinghouse are a dozen drifters from various countries of Europe and North Africa. "These people's principal possessions," he writes, "were their stories, and their stories spilled easily out of them. But I noted nothing down. I asked no questions." Nevertheless, years later in *The Mimic Men* Naipaul reached back in his memory to re-create the emotional climate of his days in Earl's Court boardinghouse.

The rest of this section briefly mentions his trips back home and to India, his writing such books as *The Middle Passage, The Loss of El Dorado,* and *In a Free State*. The emphasis, however, is always upon his state of mind and how the deepening knowledge of his past, gained in part through his studies of the history of Trinidad and his travel through and analysis of India, illuminates the lost landscapes of his ancestors while simultaneously underscoring the desolation, poverty and ruin that have befallen these worlds. It is only during his hermitage years in Wiltshire that Naipaul comes fully to realize that the perfect landscape is a private vision, a state of mind, constructed out of the natural world, but since that world and the mind that re-creates it are both constantly changing, that its beauty and harmony are able to fulfill him only for a time. In Wiltshire he discovers the great lesson of Wallace Stevens's "Sunday Morning"—"Death is the Mother of Beauty; hence from her, / Alone, shall come fulfillment to our dreams / And our desires."

The next section of the novel, "Ivy," opens with several images of decay and death amidst life. Naipaul sees a group of powerful, healthy steers on the upper slope and thinks how they are waiting now "only for the covered trailer and the trip along the winding valley road to the slaughterhouse in the town." While walking along a path he later comes upon the rotting carcass of a hare. "What mighty hind legs! Folded in death," he thinks, and this image of power and speed rendered impotent by death conjures up the picture of pelican skeletons he saw ten years earlier near Trinidad. These large birds "had folded their powerful wings and settled down to die" in a sanctuary and their bones resembled the strong hind legs of the hare.

These images of death that haunt the narrator's landscape, however, are then muted through the channels of art. Naipaul looks along the valley and sees it as "emblematic," the horses and elm stumps (another image of death), the green and the shadows all combine to form a simple and clear view, "as in a primitive painting." Looking toward the water meadows he realizes that they are "like the water meadows Constable had painted one hundred and fifty years before." A gypsy caravan parked across the road from Jack's cottage reminds him of the illustrations from *The Wind in the Willows*. The river that lies at the heart of that book seems similar to the river that passes through the manor grounds. "Shepard and Constable—they had imposed their vision on an old landscape," he observes.

As he shifts his subject from death to art and literature, Naipaul again raises one of the book's central themes—that the world changes, seems to run down, but that each person re-creates that world for himself and makes it new, only to witness his private world move toward decay. Through their works, however, the artist and writer can impose their visions upon subsequent generations even though their creative heirs eventually assimilate those visions into their own.

Naipaul repeats, as in a poetic refrain, that he saw his landlord only once—a fleeting glimpse as he was driven past him in a car—and that he never spoke to him. In fact, he takes precautions to keep his landlord at a safe distance in order to maintain his image as a mysterious recluse, an ironic sort of twin:

> I was his opposite in every way, social, artistic, sexual. And considering that his family's fortune had grown, but enormously, with the spread of the empire in the nineteenth century, it might be said that an empire lay between us. The empire at the same time linked us. The empire explained my birth in the New World, the language I used, the vocation and ambition I had; this empire in the end explained my presence there in the valley, in the cottage, in the grounds of the manor. But we were—or had started—at opposite ends of wealth, privilege, and in the hearts of different cultures. (p. 191).

These totally different men are brought together not only by the empire but by their mutual desire to escape from a painful experience in their lives. After the pride of ambition was damaged by his Boston publisher, Naipaul came to the manor for refuge, a place where he could strip his life down to its bare essentials. Similarly, his landlord had suffered some mysterious hurt in the past that led to his acedia and withdrawal from the world. "I felt at one with my landlord," Naipaul declares.

Naipaul attempts to imagine what his landlord's view of the world must be and how it is different from his own. Although spiritually weakened by personal flaws and disappointments, the landlord possesses a knowledge of his own great security. He knows who he is. His view from the manor is that of a perfect world, with nothing in it to stimulate action or encourage doubt. The view, complete and simple, seems to say: "This is the world. Why worry? Why interfere?" This attitude resembles that of Salim, in *A Bend in the River*, who opens his narrative with the observation, "The world is what it is." Unlike the poor houses of Naipaul's youth whose walls and floors trembled when one walked through them, the manor and its outbuildings were built for long use: "there was no fragility, no anxiety."

In Naipaul's view, "perfection such as my landlord looked out on contained its own corruption," and he wonders what he saw when he looked out. Was he disturbed by the wish to restore the grounds, by their lack of care and their gradual decay? Did he see the ivy that was killing the trees planted years ago? Naipaul will never know this man's perceptions, but he does know that he has discovered solace and fulfillment "in the debris of his [landlord's] garden, the debris of his own life." Although he does not use this language, one could argue that Naipaul's psychological nourishment here is parasitic in nature, that the artist is like a mushroom feeding on the detritus of his host.

Naipaul then turns his attention to Pitton, the gardener. Years ago, when the manor was at its peak of grandeur, there were sixteen gardeners. Now Pitton works among the ruins. Like Naipaul, Pitton entertains no romantic desire to see the grounds restored but is "a camper in the ruins, living with what he found." Naipaul comes to admire Pitton, his rituals and his proper dress for each season, and his vulnerability. As time passes and the expenses of running the manor mount, Pitton is finally let go. The significance of this departure is that it marks another stage in the decay of Naipaul's second childhood in Wiltshire, the deterioration of his safe house in the woods. As he says, "So quite suddenly, from one day to the next, part of the routine of the manor I had grown into, part of my new life and comfort, my private, living book of hours, was snapped."

Images of departure, dereliction, and decay continue to crowd in upon the narrator in the next section, entitled "Rooks." Alan, a literary friend of the landlord, visits Naipaul on several occasions. In him Naipaul appears to see the man he might have become, the failed writer. Although he has conducted radio interviews and discussions and has published some short essays, Alan's plans for a novel never materialize. He is a lonely and melancholy man always writing notes about people he was going to put into his novel. He braces himself in his solitude with music and alcohol. Months pass and Naipaul begins to observe Alan's changed features and manner. Then one day he hears that Alan has taken some pills after a day of hard drinking and died. And so, another departure, another assault upon Naipaul's vision of a peaceful, supportive landscape.

In a conversation with Mr. Phillips's old father, Naipaul learns that the huge flock of rooks that is disturbing the silence of the manor has been caused by the fact that they lost their nests when the elms died. They are prospecting for tall trees. These rooks become emblematic of the raucous changes that are overwhelming the land. With the death of the elms come the rooks; with the departure of Pitton come part-time workers who, in their fragmented way, attempt to carry out Pitton's methodical and unified labors. Vagrants begin to wander onto the grounds, some of whom camp there until discovered. Naipaul observes that the "order that Pitton had imposed not only on the grounds but also on my idea of the seasons, that order had gone."

When Mr. Phillips dies, the order and authority that helped hold together the life of the manor also vanish. The people who come to work in what used to be the garden are marauders and vandals. "Accidents," Naipaul says, "a whole series of accidents, had kept me protected in what was an exposed situation. Now that protection was coming to an end. The rooks building and cawing above in the beeches—perhaps this was what they had also portended." Naipaul then falls ill again with a lung infection. When he returns to his stone cottage after a stay at the hospital, he knows that his time left in the valley is quickly coming to an end. He has trained himself earlier to accept the idea of change so as to avoid grief, but, as he says, "philosophy failed me now":

> Land is not land alone, something that simply is itself. Land partakes of what we breathe into it, is touched by our moods and memories. And this end of a cycle, in my life, and in the life of the manor, mixed up with the feeling of age which my illness was forcing on me, caused me grief. (p. 335)

He acknowledges that he had always known that there was no way of preserving a landscape, one that was especially pure after his first spring in the valley, except to remember it and to record it in his writing. When that first spring unfolded its beauty and peace to him it simultaneously revealed its imminent corruption. Now he faces his own departure from the landscape, and it is like a death, a culmination of the many deaths around him over the years and of the decay and deterioration of the buildings and grounds. "And as at a death," he writes, "everything here that had been a source of pleasure and surprise, everything that had welcomed me and healed me, became a cause for pain."

In the final section of the book, "The Ceremony of Farewell," he returns to Trinidad after the death of his sister. He observes that the sacred world of his first childhood in Trinidad has long ago vanished. Every generation continues to remove him further from those holy memories. "But we remade the world for ourselves," he says. The death of his sister forced him to face his own mortality and the vanity of human wishes. And that was when, he says, "I laid aside my drafts and hesitations and began to write very fast about Jack and his garden."

This novel recapitulates and offers a tentative resolution of many of the major themes of Naipaul's previous work. His earlier obsession with sexuality and violence has become muted. He sees now how his youthful preoccupation with Angela has blinded him to the more significant subject of the mingling of cultures. In the characters of Les and Brenda, however, he depicts the destructive nature of sexuality. His limited perspective as narrator, on the other hand, keeps the passion and the violence at a great distance. He simply reports Brenda's murder matter-of-factly, as he learns of it from Mrs. Phillips. The recurrent theme of the exile seeking his home takes a new direction in this novel, as the narrator discovers his second childhood in Wiltshire and a true sense of peace and fulfillment. Within the space of ten years Naipaul gradually subdues the panic and fear that drove such characters as Mr. Biswas, Linda and Bobby, and Salim. He also discovers a new context within which to evaluate and overcome the depression and despair of Ralph Singh. In facing his own mortality and the decay of his dreams and ambitions, Naipaul has achieved a measure of fulfillment. In recreating his world anew he also comes to the painful realization that this sense of wholeness and grace must begin to fade away as soon as it is experienced. Despite the grief that decay inevitably brings, however, he has come to accept the paradoxical nature of change. Change may destroy the perfect landscape but it also offers the possibility of new landscapes. Like Mr. Biswas, who rebelled against conventional restraints in order to seek his own house, Naipaul, in *The Enigma of Arrival*, has journeyed through many painful changes to find solace, at least for a time, in his safe home in the wood.

7

A House for Mr. Naipaul

A happy, well-adjusted person usually does not become a writer. The romantic notion that a writer is someone who is driven by a private hurt or obsession seems clearly evident in the case of V. S. Naipaul. The act of writing is his means of constructing a psychological defense against the world, of imposing a sense of order upon the chaos of experience, and of securing his safe house in the wood. As Graham Greene says, "Writing is a form of therapy; sometimes I wonder how all those who do not write, compose or paint can manage to escape the madness, the melancholia, the panic fear which is inherent in the human condition."[1]

Throughout his life Naipaul has been driven by many psychological demons, and while he may have driven out one or two and restrained a few others through his prolific writings, his literary career reveals an obsession with certain themes and subjects. Fundamental to understanding all of his work is the bitterness, resentment, and rage of the failed romantic. His grandiose dreams of becoming a writer, his belief in the mythic past of his ancestors, and his great cultural expectations upon moving to England (a place he fabricated out of his infatuation with nineteenth-century British novels) set him up for the fall. These romantic fantasies were, to paraphrase Yeats, the self-born mockers of Naipaul's own youthful enterprise.

The sense of cultural deprivation that he developed as a young man in Trinidad dreaming of Dickens's snowy scenes in the London world of high culture literally drove Naipaul from his homeland to England in a desperate attempt to develop his creative talents in a society that favors literature over the rhythm of steel drums.

Ironically, the very country in which he sought refuge from the legacy of his shipwrecked ancestors was the one largely responsible for the cultural dereliction of Trinidad.

Beneath even the comedy of his early novels and stories Naipaul reveals a curious nineteenth-century sense of dislocation that recalls Matthew Arnold's painful sense that he is wandering between two worlds, one dead and one powerless to be born. Naipaul also shares Arnold's belief that life is a seriousness business full of high moral purpose and earnestness and that literature is a criticism of that life. Naipaul's Brahmin fastidiousness blends well with the puritanical ethics that he shares with the Victorian writers.

In *Miguel Street, The Mystic Masseur,* and *The Suffrage of Elvira* Naipaul depends largely upon the wit of his characters, their colorful language, and their humor as a means of distancing himself from an uncongenial world. Like the comic folk in Dickens's *Pickwick Papers,* Naipaul's islanders lack depth and complexity. Dickens, however, assumes a sophisticated British culture against which to judge and evaluate his characters. Mr. Pickwick and his cohorts may turn up in satires and parodies of British clubs, the legal system, sports, and politics but the reader is keenly aware of the great historical significance that such institutions and traditions carry in England. The reader can laugh at these characters knowing that they walk upon a solid cultural ground laid centuries ago. Naipaul's comic perspective, however, is of a different kind. The political humor in *The Suffrage of Elvira,* for example, is not viewed from within the cultural context of Trinidad but rather from outside that country, and exhibits its people in a burlesque of English politics. Both Dickens and Naipaul assume an authorial superiority over their characters in designing their comedies, but Naipaul's humor delivers the more lethal blow, because, as he well knows, he is laughing at mimic men and at what he himself might have been. He puts the political and social charades of island life behind him by writing about them, enhances an imitative culture through his comedy, and seeks his own deliverance from this exotic wasteland as a famous writer in England.

A House for Mr. Biswas remains the central novel in Naipaul's career. This intensely personal book embodies his great obsession with the need for psychological shelter. A house, one's family, independence, permanence, and identity are all mixed up in this quest. Over and over again in the novels and travel books that follow Naipaul fixes upon this obsession with place. Ralph Singh, Jimmy Ahmed, and Salim are among the many characters who suffer in their quest for inner security and peace. At home in neither their native lands nor in England, they turn to writing or violence in a desperate attempt to escape from their frustrations, anger, and pain. Naipaul expresses these powerful emotions through different characters and in different forms throughout his career. Through the characters of Richard Stone, Ralph Singh, and Mohun Biswas he shows the civilizing power of writing to bring order into their lives. Jimmy Ahmed and the narrator of "Tell Me Who to Kill," on the other hand, reveal the raw violent emotions that Naipaul carries with him. By projecting these self-destructive feelings onto madmen, Naipaul dissociates himself from their visceral response to frustration. At the same time, however, he has created forms in which to embody his own rage and to battle the panic fear that is inherent in the human condition.

As a man without a permanent home during the first forty years of his life, Naipaul at last discovered the sweet illusion of home and permanence in his Wiltshire cottage, described in *The Enigma of Arrival*. His meditation upon death and decay as the mother of beauty finally leads to his realization that his search for permanence, peace, and a sense of oneness with the world can be realized only through artistic vision. His experience of life in the valley and his meticulous recording and arrangement of particular details of the landscape and the lives of the people around him comprise that vision and afford him a shelter from his own fears.

Although a member of the British literary establishment Naipaul continues to seek out new adventures that help him to define his own past. Based upon his tour of the southern United States, his forthcoming book *A Turn in the South* should provide new insights into Southern culture and into Naipaul's own mind and character. A small section of the book has appeared in a magazine. Entitled "How the Land Lay," it tells of Naipaul's visit to Tuskegee University. Naipaul's father, who enjoyed stories of self-help and of men rising out of poverty, used to read Booker T. Washington's *Up From Slavery* to him when he was a boy. "It was hard to forget that story," he says: "the fairy-tale test, the doing of a seemingly trivial or irrelevant thing extremely well."[2]

Naipaul reports on the memories of oldtimers who attended the university. The general thrust of these accounts and of Naipaul's observations is that Tuskegee offered blacks an oasis during a period when they had no where else to turn. The school provided a congenial intellectual and social atmosphere, but more importantly, it gave blacks the opportunity to learn a trade. Unlike W. E. B. Du Bois, who, according to Naipaul, indulged in lyricism for its own sake and harbored a sentimental obsession with Africa, Booker T. Washington was convinced that the American black could not improve his lot by emigrating to Africa. Instead of relying upon empty rhetoric, Washington set forth a practical program of education for blacks, one that lured and nourished the scientific genius of George Washington Carver.

Beneath the reportage, the anecdotes, and the quotations that comprise this piece one may detect Naipaul's personal fascination with Tuskegee, and the reason for his going there. During the period of segregation in America this school provided sanctuary in Alabama: "Many of the people I met had been at Tuskegee for much of their lives. And, though this might have been fortuitous, many of the old residents were light-skinned, some of them almost white; courtly, polished people, who would have been dreadfully wounded by the indignities of the world outside, and even now, in their old age, didn't wish to drop their guard" (p. 98).

Tuskegee appears to be, then, another embodiment of Naipaul's recurrent symbol of the safe house. Like Mr. Biswas's house and like his own cottage in Wiltshire, this place protected one from the cruel social and psychological pressures that threatened to kill the human spirit. Naipaul's conclusion to this chapter, however, suggests that this glorious sanctuary has served its purpose and now seems like a relic from the past, a prison from which another generation has now escaped: "From the NASA museum, full of Asian visitors . . . — Tuskegee seemed to belong to another age, to exist in a melancholy time warp. It made one think of the prisons of the spirit that men create for themselves and for others—so overpowering, so much a part of the way things appear to have to be, and then, abruptly, with a little shift, so insubstantial" (p. 105).

A Turn in the South and other books yet to come may reveal new aspects to Naipaul's obsessions. At this point, however, the rootless wanderer has built himself a house of words, of books, each one providing a temporary shelter. And so he will continue to re-create new landscapes, new symbols of enclosure, as time renders previous ones insubstantial.

Notes

1. The World as It Is

1. "The Novelist V. S. Naipaul Talks to Nigel Bingham about His Childhood in Trinidad," *Listener,* Sept. 7, 1972, p. 306.
2. Ibid.
3. Kenneth Ramchand, *The West Indian Novel and its Background* (New York: Barnes & Noble, 1970), pp. 189–90.
4. "The Novelist V. S. Naipaul Talks to Nigel Bingham about His Childhood in Trinidad," p. 307.
5. Ibid.
6. Ibid.
7. M. Banning Eyre, "Naipaul at Wesleyan," *South Carolina Review* 14 (Spring 1982): 34–47.
8. "A Conversation with V. S. Naipaul," *Salmagundi* 54 (Fall 1981): 4–22. Interview conducted at Wesleyan University in May of 1979 by Bharati Mukherjee and Robert Boyers.
9. Ibid., p. 5.
10. Eyre, "Naipaul at Wesleyan," p. 46.

2. The Comic Island

1. John Thieme, "Calypso Allusions in Naipaul's *Miguel Street,*" *Kunapipi* 3, no. 2 (1981): 25.
2. Ibid., p. 27.
3. V. S. Naipaul, *Miguel Street* (New York: Vintage Books, 1984), p. 90.
4. Mukherjee and Boyers, "A Conversation with V. S. Naipaul," *Salmagundi* 54 (Fall 1981): 7.
5. Robert D. Hamner, *V. S. Naipaul* (New York: Twayne Publishers, 1973), p. 32.
6. "V. S. Naipaul," *Times,* Jan. 2, 1964, p. 11.
7. V. S. Naipaul, *The Mystic Masseur* (New York: Vintage Books, 1984), p. 79. Hereafter cited as *MM.*
8. V. S. Naipaul, "Writing Is Magic," *Sunday Times,* Nov. 10, 1968, p. 57.

9. Quoted by Naipaul in "The Regional Barrier," *Times Literary Suplement,* Aug. 15, 1958, pp. 37–38; reprinted in *Critical Perspectives on V. S. Naipaul,* ed. Robert D. Hamner (Washington, DC: Three Continents Press, 1977), p. 7.
10. Ibid.
11. Kerry McSweeney, *Four Contemporary Novelists* (Kingston and Montreal: McGill-Queen's University Press, 1983), p. 165.
12. Quoted by M. Banning Eyre in "Naipaul at Wesleyan," *South Carolina Review* 14 (Spring 1982): 42.
13. Peter Nazareth, " 'The Mimic Men' as a Study of Corruption," in *Critical Perspectives on V. S. Naipaul,* ed. Robert D. Hamner (Washington, DC: Three Continents Press, 1977), pp. 144–45.
14. Ibid., p. 152.

3. Breaking Away

1. V. S. Naipaul, *A House for Mr. Biswas* (New York: Vintage Books, 1984), pp. 13–14. Hereafter cited as *HMB.*
2. Ramchand, *The West Indian Novel and Its Background* (New York: Barnes & Noble, 1970), p. 192.
3. Gordon Rohlehr, "The Ironic Approach: The Novels of V. S. Naipaul," in *Critical Perspectives on V. S. Naipaul,* ed. Robert D. Hamner (Washington, DC: Three Continents Press, 1977), p. 190.
4. Ramchand, *The West Indian Novel and Its Background,* p. 201.
5. Ibid., p. 204.
6. Rohlehr, "The Ironic Approach: The Novels of V. S. Naipaul," pp. 192–93.
7. William Walsh, *V. S. Naipaul* (New York: Barnes & Noble, 1973), pp. 42–44.
8. V. S. Naipaul, *Finding the Center* (New York: Knopf, 1984), p. 72.
9. Robert D. Hamner, *V. S. Naipaul* (New York: Twayne, 1973), p. 89.
10. Ibid.
11. Kerry McSweeney, *Four Contemporary Novelists* (Kingston and Montreal: McGill-Queen's University Press, 1983), p. 171.
12. Rohlehr, "The Ironic Approach: The Novels of V. S. Naipaul," pp. 187–88.

4. Shipwrecked

1. V. S. Naipaul, *The Middle Passage* (New York: Vintage Books, 1981), p. 9. Hereafter cited as *MP.*
2. Mukherjee and Boyers, "A Conversation with V. S. Naipaul," *Salmagundi* 54 (Fall 1981): 13.
3. "V. S. Naipaul," *Times,* Jan. 2, 1964, p. 11.
4. V. S. Pritchett, "Climacteric," *New Statesman,* May 31, 1963, p. 831.
5. "V. S. Naipaul," *Times,* Jan. 2, 1964, p. 11.
6. V. S. Naipaul, *Mr. Stone and the Knights Companion* (New York, Vintage Books, 1985), p. 118. Hereafter cited as *KC.*
7. Pritchett, "Climacteric," *New Statesman,* May 31, 1963, p. 832.

8. V. S. Naipaul, *A Flag on the Island* (London: Andre Deutsch, 1967), p. 149. Hereafter cited as *FI*.
9. V. S. Naipaul, "Writing Is Magic," *Sunday Times*, Nov. 10, 1968, p. 57.
10. Israel Shenker, "V. S. Naipaul, Man without a Society," *New York Times Book Review*, Oct. 17, 1971, p. 22.
11. V. S. Naipaul, *The Mimic Men* (New York: Vintage Books, 1985), p. 18. Hereafter cited as *MM*.
12. V. S. Naipaul, *An Area of Darkness* (New York: Vintage Books, 1981), p. 45. Hereafter cited as *AD*.
13. V. S. Naipaul, "Writing Is Magic," *Sunday Times*, November 10, 1968, p. 57.
14. John Wain, "Trouble in the Family," *New York Review of Books*, Oct. 26, 1967, pp. 34–35.
15. V. S. Naipaul, "Writing Is Magic," *Sunday Times*, Nov. 10, 1968, p. 57.
16. "Portrait of an Artist: What Makes Naipaul Run," *Caribbean Contact* 1 (May 6, 1973): 18.
17. John Thieme, "V. S. Naipaul and the Hindu Killer," *Journal of Indian Writing in English*, July 9, 1981, p. 73.
18. V. S. Naipaul, "London," reprinted in *The Overcrowded Barracoon* (New York: Vintage Books, 1984), p. 16.
19. Thieme, "V. S. Naipaul and the Hindu Killer," p. 78.

5. Landscapes of Fear

1. V. S. Naipaul, *In a Free State* (New York: Vintage Books, 1984), pp. 57–58. Hereafter cited as *IFS*.
2. Mukhergee and Boyers, "A Conversation with V. S. Naipaul," *Salmagundi* 54 (Fall 1981): 19.
3. Ibid.
4. V. S. Naipaul, *The Enigma of Arrival* (New York: Knopf, 1987), p. 99. Hereafter cited as *EA*.
5. Angus Calder, "Darkest Naipaulia," *New Statesman*, Oct. 8, 1971, p. 483.
6. Mukhergee and Boyers, "A Conversation with V. S. Naipaul," *Salmagundi* 54 (Fall 1981): 16.
7. V. S. Naipaul, *Guerrillas* (New York: Vintage Books, 1980), p. 144.
8. V. S. Naipaul, "Violence in Art: The Documentary Heresy," *Twentieth Century* 173 (Winter 1964 / 65): 107.
9. Ibid., p. 108.
10. Mukhergee and Boyers, "A Conversation with V. S. Naipaul," *Salmagundi* 54 (Fall 1981): p. 16.
11. John Updike, *"Un Pé Pourrie," New Yorker*, May 21, 1979, p. 141.
12. Ibid.
13. Elaine Campbell, "A Refinement of Rage: V. S. Naipaul's *A Bend in the River*," *World Literature Written in English*, 18 (Spring 1981): 399.
14. V. S. Naipaul, *A Bend in the River* (New York: Vintage Books, 1980), p. 272. Hereafter cited as *BR*.

6. A Safe House in the Wood

1. Paul Theroux, *V. S. Naipaul: An Introduction to his Work* (New York: Africana Publishing Corp., 1972), p. 15.
2. Review of *The Enigma of Arrival, Booklist,* Jan. 15, 1987, p. 729.
3. Review of *The Enigma of Arrival, Publishers' Weekly,* Jan. 23, 1987, p. 62.
4. Paul Gray, "The Gift of a Second Life," *Time,* March 2, 1987, p. 75.
5. Christopher Lehmann-Haupt, "Books of the Times," *New York Times,* March 5, 1987, p. 24C.
6. Jay Tolson, "Naipaul's 'Arrival' at Self-discovery," *USA Today,* March 6, 1987, p. 7D.
7. V. S. Naipaul, "On Being a Writer," *New York Review of Books,* April 23, 1987, p. 7.
8. Ibid.
9. V. S. Naipaul, *The Enigma of Arrival* (New York: Knopf, 1987), p. 344. Hereafter cited as *EA.*

7. A House for Mr. Naipaul

1. Graham Greene, *Ways of Escape* (New York: Washington Square Press, 1980), p. vii.
2. V. S. Naipaul, "Reflections / How the Land Lay," *New Yorker,* June 6, 1988, p. 94. Subsequent page references will be indicated in the text.

Bibliography

Books by Naipaul

(Arranged according to date of original publication, noted in brackets)

The Mystic Masseur. New York: Vintage Books, 1984. [1957]
The Suffrage of Elvira. New York: Vintage Books, 1985. [1958]
Miguel Street. New York: Vintage Books, 1984. [1959]
A House for Mr. Biswas. New York: Vintage Books, 1984. [1961]
The Middle Passage. New York: Vintage Books, 1981. [1962]
Mr. Stone and the Knights Companion. New York: Vintage Books, 1985. [1963]
An Area of Darkness. New York: Vintage Books, 1981. [1964]
The Mimic Men. New York: Vintage Books, 1985. [1967]
A Flag on the Island. London: Andre Deutsch, 1967.
The Loss of El Dorado. New York: Vintage Books, 1984. [1970]
In a Free State. New York: Vintage Books, 1984. [1971]
The Overcrowded Barracoon. New York: Vintage Books, 1984. [1972]
Guerrillas. New York: Vintage Books, 1980. [1975]
India: A Wounded Civilization. New York: Vintage Books, 1978. [1977]
A Bend in the River. New York: Vintage Books, 1980. [1979]
The Return of Eva Peron with the Killings in Trinidad. New York: Vintage Books, 1981. [1980]
Among the Believers. London: Andre Deutsch, 1981.
Finding the Center. New York: Knopf, 1984.
The Enigma of Arrival. New York: Knopf, 1987.
A Turn in the South. New York: Knopf, 1989 [forthcoming]

Selected Essays by Naipaul

"The Regional Barrier." *Times Literary Supplement,* Aug. 15, 1958, pp. 37–38.
"When I Was a Kid." *New Statesman,* Dec. 22, 1961, p. 963.
"Speaking of Writing." *Times,* Jan. 2, 1964, p. 11.
"Words of Their Own." *Times Literary Supplement,* June 4, 1964, p. 472.

"Violence in Art: The Documentary Heresy." *Twentieth Century*, 173 (Winter 1964/65): 107–8.
"The Writer." *New Statesman*, March 18, 1966, p. 381.
"What's Wrong with Being a Snob?" *Saturday Evening Post*, 240 (June 3, 1967): 12, 18.
"Writing Is Magic." *Sunday Times*, Nov. 10, 1968, p. 57.
"On Being a Writer." *New York Review of Books*, April 23, 1987, p. 7.
"Reflections / How the Land Lay." *New Yorker*, June 6, 1988, pp. 94–105.

Selected Interviews

"V. S. Naipaul." *Sunday Times Magazine*, May 26, 1963, p. 13. [With David Bates]
"V. S. Naipaul." *Times*, Jan. 2, 1964, p. 11.
Sunday Times, Sept. 10, 1968. [With Francis Wyndham]
"Without a Place." *Times Literary Supplement*, July 30, 1971, pp. 897–98. [With Ian Hamilton]
"V. S. Naipaul: Man without a Society." *New York Times Book Review*, Oct. 17, 1971, pp. 22–24. [With Israel Shenker]
"The Novelist V. S. Naipaul Talks about His Childhood in Trinidad." *Listener*, Sept. 7, 1972, pp. 306–7. [With Nigel Bingham]
"The Novelist V. S. Naipaul Talks about His Work." *Listener*, March 22, 1973, pp. 367–68, 370. [With Ronald Bryden]
"Portrait of an Artist: What Makes Naipaul Run." *Caribbean Contact*, 1 (May 6, 1973): 18.
"A Conversation with V. S. Naipaul." *Salmagundi* 54 (Fall 1981): 4–22. [At Wesleyan University in May of 1979 with Bharati Mukherjee and Robert Boyers]

Critical Studies

Calder, Angus. "Darkest Naipaulia." *New Statesman*, Oct. 8, 1971, p. 483.
Campbell, Elaine. "A Refinement of Rage: V. S. Naipaul's *A Bend in the River*." *World Literature Written in English*, 18 (Spring 1981): 394–406.
The Enigma of Arrival book review. *Booklist*, Jan. 15, 1987, p. 729.
The Enigma of Arrival book review. *Publishers' Weekly*, Jan. 23, 1987, p. 62.
Eyre, M. Banning. "Naipaul at Wesleyan." *South Carolina Review* 14 (Spring 1982): 34–47.
Gray, Paul. "The Gift of a Second Life." Review of *The Enigma of Arrival*. *Time*, March 2, 1987, p. 75.
Hamner, Robert D. *V. S. Naipaul*. New York: Twayne Publishers, 1973.
____, ed. *Critical Perspectives on V. S. Naipaul*. Washington, DC: Three Continents Press, 1977.
Lehmann-Haupt, Christopher. "Books of the Times." Review of *The Enigma of Arrival*. March 5, 1987, p. 24C.
McSweeney, Kerry. *Four Contemporary Novelists*. Kingston and Montreal: McGill-Queen's University Press, 1983.

Nazareth, Peter. " 'The Mimic Men' as a Study of Corruption." Reprinted in *Critical Perspectives on V. S. Naipaul,* ed. Robert D. Hamner. Washington, DC: Three Continents Press, 1977.

Pritchett, V.S. "Climacteric." *New Statesman,* May 31, 1963, p. 831.

Ramchand, Kenneth. *The West Indian Novel and Its Background.* New York: Barnes & Noble, 1970.

Rohlehr, Gordon. "The Ironic Approach: The Novels of V. S. Naipaul." Reprinted in *Critical Perspectives on V. S. Naipaul,* ed. Robert D. Hamner. Washington, DC: Three Continents Press, 1977.

Theroux, Paul. *V. S. Naipaul: An Introduction to his Work.* New York: Africana Publishing Corp., 1972.

Thieme, John. "Calypso Allusions in Naipaul's *Miguel Street.*" *Kunapipi* 3, no. 2 (1981): 18–32.

———. "V. S. Naipaul and the Hindu Killer." *Journal of Indian Writing in English,* July 9, 1981, pp. 70–86.

Thorp, Michael. *V. S. Naipaul.* Edinburgh. Longman Group Ltd., 1976.

Tolson, Jay. "Naipaul's 'Arrival' at Self-discovery." *USA Today,* March 6, 1987, p. 7D.

Updike, John. *"Un Pé Pourrie."* *New Yorker,* May 21, 1979, pp. 141–44.

Wain, John. "Trouble in the Family." *New York Review of Books,* Oct. 26, 1967, pp. 33–35.

Walsh, William, *V. S. Naipaul.* New York: Barnes & Noble, 1973.

White, Landeg. *V. S. Naipaul: A Critical Introduction.* London: Macmillan, 1975.

Index